CAUGHT UP

Night Vision Revealed

Mark D Watt

MDW & BPW Media

Caught Up Night Vision Revealed

ISBN: 0615891454
ISBN-13: 978-0615891453 - (MDW & BPW Media)

Dedication

First, and foremost I thank God for the spiritual gifts He has bestowed in me: prophetic insight, discernment, a word of wisdom, a word of knowledge, etc., and the ability to think, to be creative, to have ideas, and to see those things manifest into existence. If it were not for God leading and guiding me this book would not be possible.

The dedication of this book is to my Mother (Gloria Watt) and my aunt (Helen Lambert) who played major roles in my life. My mother would always say ... "keep running and never look back". She instilled a lot of wisdom in me and I still carry that wisdom today. Yes, I miss my mother and my aunt very much. My aunt Helen filled the void my mother left after she passed away in May of 1980. I thank the Lord for the Night Vision revealed to me, so that it would prepare people of what is to come and to share with all who will believe it and receive it.

Contents

Forward

Very informative and realistic book unlike the normal books you will find on End-Of-The-Church-Age. As I was reading, I continuously stayed on the edge of my seat. Not so much because of the anticipation one might get by reading a mystery book, but instead, kept on the edge of my seat because of the interest the book had on my attention. "Would you like to know more"? These words kept me seeking more. I wanted to know more about the vision God himself had given to the man of God in a dream. I wanted to explore with him what God had shown him. That is what this book does! It keeps you wanting to know more.

The book has scriptures to back it up and support everything taking place. I love how the author breaks down the Scripture so that the understanding is clear enough for everyone to receive revelation to it. The way the Bible says in the book of Revelation of how the "Rapture" or "Catching Away" will take place and how the vision God has shown the Prophet are so closely alike. I recommend this book to both believers of God as well as non-believers.

- Evangelist Rebecca Porter-Watt

Acknowledgments

First, I give honor to and acknowledge God and my LORD and Savior Jesus Christ who is the final authority in my life. In addition, to my wife Evangelist Rebecca Porter-Watt who continued to encourage me, especially too complete this book, and how the time is right for this true prophetic night vision revealed too me on December 8, 2008 to come forth right now in this time and season we are currently in. I thank you so very, very much!

Those of you that are reading this book, believe, and receive what is pertained here, spread the word about it and share socially. With your assistance, we can wake people up from the sleep the enemy has them walking in. I thank you in advance as well.

Daniel 12:9 KJV

And he said, Go thy way, Daniel: for the words are closed up and sealed till the time of the end.

Introduction

BEFORE I BEGIN, I want to elaborate for a minute on the "*I do not believe* Generation Y", and what the Bible says regarding this generation. First, there are many prophecies in the Bible that say it shall "come to pass" of unparalleled calamity, financial meltdown, destruction and an "apocalyptic" event that will sweep across this planet. First, known as the "Rapture" or "Caught Up" secondly the "Tribulation Period" and the loss of life will be so great in all the land, nearly all the inhabitants of the earth will perish. One would think the bleak nature of these future events would cause people to have a wake-up call, and to be forever mindful of these events. It is sad to say, that only a small percentage of the population truly believes, and is paying attention to the signs of the times concerning End-Of-The-Church-Age and God's prophetic agenda. I believe it is safe to say that ignorance, lack of information or shortage of resources to obtain the truth of Bible prophecy is not the root cause of the problem, but disobedience to the written Word of God is truly the root cause. As we look at where we are in this time, we can see evidence of the comprising of the Word of God in today's New Testament living. Yes, there are groups of people in remote areas on this planet that are not familiar with Jesus Christ. However, it says… "[14]*And this gospel of the kingdom shall be preached in all the world for a witness unto all nations; and then shall the end come.*" Matthew 24:14 KJV – Based on this scripture, those people in remote areas and all over the world will eventually get the Gospel, the "Good

News." All I can say is listen up and get your head out of the sand you "*I do not believe* Generation Y". I have not been on this earth for a long number of years, but as I read what the Bible says and observe the signs of the times, I have never seen so much evidence that points to the return of the second coming of Jesus Christ. Yes, we are definitely witnessing the last days! The evidence of prophecy-related events clearly shows that our lease agreement on this present day earth is almost at its end and I strongly believe that this generation will witness the dawn of the "Kingdom Age" come to pass.

As I reflect on the prophet Isaiah and the prophet Daniel, and how God revealed to them various dreams and visions of what is to come. I see myself in this same position. They had many divine visitations from the Lord thy God, as I continue to experience the same divine visitations, and that experience is tantamount to divine revelation. It is because of the presence of God is key to the dream and vision realm. When we explore the Bible, it has revealed many times in the past and present to his servants; prophets of God dreams and visions for specific reasons to convey special messages at the appointed time to themselves, individuals or to a group of people of the local Church and the nations. Since God did this in the past, He is doing it now (presently), and for the future. I say this because it is an accurate statement, if one were a true prophet operating under the Old Testament, the prophet Jeremiah says in Jeremiah 23:18 (*For who hath stood in the counsel of the LORD,…*). The New Testament replaces this; which is the Day of Pentecost caught the entire Church up because of the Holy Spirit divine council. Just like the prophet Jeremiah of the Old

Testament, I bring a warning to you of what is to come forth in the earth by a prophetic voice, but through a night vision!

Would you like to know more?

The Prophetic Agenda

The scene is already set prophetically. So, where are we currently in this season, called God's true prophetic agenda? Many of you most likely are asking this question, and it is; what is (The Prophetic Agenda)? It is the truth of the Word of God behind world history and it is the fulfillment of God's prophetic purpose on His prophetic time clock; because "*God did not come out of time, time came out of Him*". There will be many, who will question, (what is the truth)? All I can say, is this is what the Word of God says… One of the things is that in biblical history God challenged His people to read the signs of the times and seasons. As we draw near the End-Of-The-Church-Age, it is extremely vital that we know which season we are currently living in right now, and discern what the Lord thy God is doing on the earth, in the earth, in the spirit realm and His purpose for the future. Why is this time and season of God's governmental perfection, order, authority and man's governmental order and authority called a prophetic agenda in the year 2012? Did you catch it? The significance is in the numbers, (2012 – twenty meaning redemption, and 12-governmental perfection and authority, God's true order). As one observes man's governmental perfection, authority and order, he truly demonstrated that it was not in order. However, the truth should catapult you into "*preparation*" for what is to come in the year 2013. Because the true prophetic Word of God since the beginning of time is now awaken in those who have discerned it in the dimension of the spirit realm and the prophetic realm. If you are able to see it, and the operation of it, it jumps off the pages of our instruction manual called (The Basic Instructions Before

Leaving Earth). This realm is a realm seen with spiritual eyes and heard with spiritual ears (the seer, visions, dreams, prophetic strategies, and a right now prophetic rhema word). The prophetic agenda connects the spiritual realm to the natural realm. Prophetically speaking, this prophetic event and message is supernatural communication in a night vision from the Lord bringing forth warning of what is to come in the future. The revelation or uncovering of it is very prevalent right now! The prophetic realm or dimension is known as the Holy Spirit or the Spirit of God which is prophetic, and He brings revelation, the mysteries, the secret things and the hidden things revealed too his true men and women of God. Watch and see!

The Prophetic Time Clock

Tick tock, tick tock, tick tock, are you observing it, can you see that it never stops? Yes, I am referring too God's prophetic time clock. Nevertheless, it is always in motion, moving forward and never stopping and it cannot be turned back by man, as much as he would like too, but it can be redeemed to a certain extent through and by the Lord thy God. Here it is right here, it was set in motion from the beginning of time and will continue for eternity… as stated earlier "*God did not come out of time, time came out of Him*", tick tock, tick tock, tick tock…The title in the next paragraph is appropriate, so "It Begins"…

It Begins

Here it is right here, even before the "rapture" or the "catching away"... the Lord our God can come for any one of us at any time - "*Watch therefore: for ye know not what hour your Lord doth come...Therefore be ye also ready*: *for in such an hour as ye think not the Son of man cometh.*" Matthew 24:42, 44 KJV - As one begins to read this book, there is a very good possibility that what I am about to share with you may be believable to some people but unbelievable to most people. This will include non-believers of Jesus Christ and possibly believers of Jesus Christ regarding end time prophecy. Most importantly, what the Bible says about the "Catching away", and even "visions and dreams". There will be a few Pastors, Ministers, Evangelists, and Preachers, etc. that will say that God does not speak to men and women of God in visions and dreams anymore. Well, I beg to differ, because in the New Testament the Book of Acts 2:17 and 18 says otherwise. They will say, He only speaks and reveals Himself to us through the written Word of God or maybe the Holy Spirit if they have any belief in that. I know there are a lot of controversies, misinterpretations, inaccurate teachings, and contradictions of the rapture as well. Yes, there are many people, and religious groups who do not believe in the "rapture" or "caught up", the tribulation or believe it will happen or apply in this day and time. I must also add that the word "rapture" is not in the Bible per-say, but the definition of it is. The word "rapture", is not found anywhere in the King James Version of the English Bible, but it is found in the Vulgate, the Latin translation of the Bible, where it is translated from the Greek word that means "caught up," or "carry off". In addition to this, the word "caught up" is (Gr. *harpazō*, "to seize", "snatch"): The Latin word for "carry off" is *raptus*, from which we get rapture. For a clear understanding in the spirit, read the following scripture... "[17]*Then we which are alive and remain shall be caught up together with them in the clouds, to meet the Lord in the air: and so shall we ever be with the Lord.*" First Thessalonians 4:17 KJV

If the "rapture," or "caught up" and the tribulation is not true, or is not going to happen, but there are various religious groups that use a Bible in their congregation; my question is what are they reading and what revelation or understanding are they receiving from it when it comes to the "rapture" or being "caught up"? I must also say that some religious groups do not use a Bible in their congregation at all, if this is the type of Church you are attending, I recommend you run quickly! What I have written in this book and what I am about to share with you may be ridiculed, have skepticism, disbelief or maybe some people will say that you must have been watching television or reading a book on the rapture and that is the reason why the dream took place. Well, I am here to share with you that this true "tell-a-vision" or night vision occurrence did take place and that I was not just an observer but also a participant. Well, it is OK if anyone that reads this book about this true night vision and does not believe it; because what I am about to share with you is so profound and true that it scared me to the point of not wanting to go back to sleep that morning or for a couple of days after it happened. However, before I expound on this true prophetic night vision, I want to enlighten you on a few truths, facts and a background on prophetic visions and dreams. The title of this book is "*Caught Up Night Vision Revealed*" and I believe it is a fitting title because ready or not, He "Jesus Christ the

Messiah, the Anointed One, the Son of man" will return, and there will be those who will be "caught up" in a blink of an eye!

This shall "come to pass" or "happen" and there is nothing we can do about it, accept for preparing oneself for His Second Coming! Would you like a few clues and truths of where we are in the time-line of Bible prophecy? If so, read on!

Would you like to know more?

The Time Line Rapture Bible Prophecy

Before the end comes, the gospel is preached all over the world

New Testament time frame -
Bible Prophecy: Matthew 24:14 KJV
Prophecy Written: First century
Future Prophecy: At the End-Of The-Church-Age
It says in... "[14]*And this gospel of the kingdom shall be preached in all the world for a witness unto all nations; and then shall the end come.*" See Matthew 24:14 KJV - Verse-14 "*then shall the end come*", would refer to the end of the Church Age. However, we are not quite there yet regarding the end. We also see in Verse-36 *"But of that day and hour knoweth no man, no, not the angels of heaven, but my Father only."*

Bible Prophecy: Acts 20:24 KJV
Prophecy Written: First century
Fulfilling Prophecy: Right now, during the current Grace Period
It says in... *"[24] But none of these things move me, neither count I my life dear unto myself, so that I might finish my course with joy, and the ministry, which I have received of the Lord Jesus, to testify the gospel of the grace of God."* See Acts 20:24 KJV

It is true that the preaching of the gospel throughout the world for a long time has come forth, as it is now. However, with the increasing worldwide availability of communication satellites around the globe, 24-hour a day television, the Internet, and now smart-phones there is greater potential for the gospel preached to everyone, everywhere as we see the evidence of this happening NOW! Today portions of or the entire Bible is translated into many languages, dialects and what I believe covers most of the world's population. What one must understand that when one reads the scriptures before this verse, one will see what season we are truly experiencing? I recommend reading the following scriptures in Matthew 24:1-44 KJV – Note: Read all of Chapter 24 in the Book of Matthew.

Would you like to know more?

A True Night Vision Appeared

The question is does God still speak to true men and women of God through visions and dreams? The answer to this question is yes! We all have the capability to have visions and dreams; I believe it is a gift from God. It does not matter if those visions or dreams are bad ones or good ones. However, not all dreams are from God. Nevertheless, there is something special that God provides to those who are his chosen and that something special is "prophetic visions" and or "prophetic dreams". Visions and prophetic dreaming are common events of a prophet. So what is the definition of "prophetic dreams or visions"? A prophetic dream is a dream that depicts facets of future events that are coming or what is about to happen. A prophetic dream is a revelation or a vision. One major characteristic often associated with these types of dreams is its vividness and distinct attention to details. These kinds of dreams have a way of being able to stay in ones memory longer compared to ordinary dreams. Just like the many prophets in the Old Testament God spoke to numerous men through "prophetic dreams" and "prophetic visions", such as King Solomon, Isaiah, Ezekiel, Samuel, and Daniel and others. In the Old Testament, several Hebrew words pertain to visions and dreams. They are…

- Ra'ah – The prophet is the seer. This form of prophetic communication the prophet receives is revelation through dreams, visions, etc. He not only sees, he hears when it comes before him.

- Chozeh – This is another form of prophetic communication of the prophet, which comes through beholding of open visions. I believe it is the highest form of prophetic communication.

However, we must not forget (Nabi – which means prophet or spokesperson for God and prophetic communication through hearing the word of the Lord in one's spirit). The visions and dreams that God revealed to these men were astounding, they revealed what was asked for, such as wisdom, truth of what has happened, and what will happen, or "come to pass" very soon. Before I move on regarding this night vision occurrence, I want to first look at the prophet Isaiah referred to as the "Prince of Prophets" and set the stage of what I will be sharing with you throughout this book, and tap into some of his insight and prophetic ministry regarding dreams. What I am going to expound on is one of his prophetic gifts, entitled the many dreams that God showed him. One of the many things I believe that took place with Isaiah is that he stated one must go through a "test the spirits" in Isaiah 8:19, 20 KJV - experience to make sure that the person who is sharing what they claim to be a prophetic Word of God or even a prophetic dream is a valid prophet of God. The life style of the prophet Isaiah is not of sin or rebellion, but obedience to the written Word of God because it was the final authority in his life. He also had a very close relationship with God and his message did not contradict the written Word of God, and he heard His voice clearly.

Therefore, what is one of the things that Isaiah did as a true prophet of God? The prophet Isaiah was a "seer" in which the physical eyes or mind cannot see. A person, who prophesies future events, has spiritual insight, and knowledge, a wise person or sage who possesses intuitive power. Overall, he was a spiritual "tell-a-vision" prophet that delivered God's messages on point with a "come to pass" or it "shall happen" results. This was extremely powerful in the Old Testament prophets such as Isaiah, and is today in real prophets that have this same gift of prophetic visions and dreams of our time! In today's New Testament, reading the written Word of God says… *"And it shall come to pass in the last days, saith God, I will pour out of my Spirit upon all flesh: and your sons and your daughters shall prophesy, and your young men shall see visions, and your old men shall dream dreams:"* Acts 2:17 KJV. What was one of the prophetic visions and or dreams that Isaiah brought forth from God? He saw… *"The vision of Isaiah the son of Amoz, which he saw concerning Judah and Jerusalem in the days of Uzziah, Jotham, Ahaz, and Hezekiah, kings of Judah."* Isaiah 1:1 KJV – The prophet Isaiah saw a *vision* (*chazōn*) a divine revelation in the spirit realm, and he received a vision from God and *foretold* the coming of the Messiah. The key words in the previous sentences are the words (vision) and (foretold) the coming of something that shall "come to pass".

Secondly, we will now seek the insight of the prophet Daniel, a man of God with the gift of prophetic visions and dreams. In addition to this, his gift includes the ability to interpret these visions and dreams with detail and on-point interpretation. He could see into the future of things to come! He was one of four children mentioned that God blessed with various prophetic gifts, but Daniel had understanding of all visions and dreams which stood out. Read Daniel 1:17 KJV. I must say this; there are some religious and non-religious groups, which question the Book of Daniel and its authenticity and credibility regarding end-time prophecies. I for one believe the prophecies that took place in the Old Testament period, and are taking place right now in the New Testament period by this awesome Man of God and prophet based on his "in the future" visions. One of the many reasons is there is a connection with what he prophesied regarding the last days and or end-times, and the night vision God revealed to me. What is one of the many key visions, dreams, or prophecies that God revealed to the prophet Daniel that "came to pass"? Well, one of today's best-known prophecies is the rise of the Antichrist and the Battle of Armageddon that the prophet Daniel recorded in sixth century B.C. The prophet Daniel wrote his prophecies during the seventy years that the people of Israel were captives or held in bondage in the land of Babylon. So first, let us start with the dream of King Nebuchadnezzar. This is the first prophecy that occurs in the Book of Daniel because chapter two sets the stage or framework for the rest of the prophecies. In this chapter, Daniel reveals the interpretation of the night vision that troubled King Nebuchadnezzar with astounding revelation. However, one of the most important wise decisions that Daniel made, is that *he requested time before the interpretation.* The prophet Daniel went to his house and brought the dream before his companions (Hananiah, Mishael, and Azariah known as the three Hebrew boys) and they prayed that God would reveal the secret before interpreting it before King Nebuchadnezzar Daniel 2:16-19 KJV: Would you like to know more? If so, I recommend reading the Book of Daniel, Chapter 2. I highly recommend that you read the entire Book of Daniel in order to get revelation and understanding.

In The Book of Daniel - Chapter 2

King Nebuchadnezzar's Night vision Breakdown

Verse 1 - King Nebuchadnezzar's request
Verse 8 - King Nebuchadnezzar's anger at the failure of the wise men
Verse 14 – Daniel's assistance is requested
Verse 16 – Daniel given time
Verse 17 - Prayer with his companions
Verse 19 - The secret revealed to Daniel in a night vision
Verse 24 - Daniel brought before the King Nebuchadnezzar
Verse 27 - Daniel clarifies that God reveals secrets
Verse 31 - The dream great image revealed
Verse 37 - The interpretation of the dream
Verse 46 - Promotion of Daniel and his companions

Is there more to the visions and dreams that Daniel had when it comes to the end-time prophecy? The answer to this question is yes! There is quite a bit to write about regarding the gifts that God bestowed upon Daniel, but this book is not about the prophet Daniel, but about the parallels of what I experienced, and the prophet Daniel experienced and what is on the horizon for us, and the prophecies to come forth in these times. Do you remember what it says in Acts 2:17 and 18? If not, then go back and read it again. I mentioned earlier that most people would have a hard time believing what I am writing; most will say another Jesus Christ is coming back prophecy, or another end of the world or end-time book. Most will say I heard it all before tell me something that I do not know; well this is what I am doing. First, I am providing you a prophetic base of visions and dreams and then present to you details and truths of various prophets that had visions and dreams. If you do not take heed to this or any other true and authentic end-time book written by true men and women of God, then you should. There are so many signs that are taking place around us; one must really wake up to this in the spirit realm and the natural realm. I for one would rather be prepared for this than not be prepared. So what are the preparations? Well the answer to this question is simple align your lifestyle up with the written Word of God. Many will not adhere to this warning, and that is a decision and choice that all of us will have to deal with! I made this statement before in a previous book, and I am going to continue to say it. As for the prophet Daniel, he is one of the Major Prophets where his visions and dreams are now "happening" at this point-in-time. His spiritual insights are truly the "writings on the wall".

Therefore, this is a time of true prophetic visions and dreams and a revealing of end-time prophecies that the Bible mentions to come forth as we see evidence of this happening right now before our very eyes. It is a major topic of discussion on television documentaries, the internet, books and on radio talk shows and even in the movies because it is more prevalent today than ever before. God has a way and or means to speak to us by getting our attention and one of those ways is through "prophetic visions and dreams" and the manifestation of them, and with "come to pass" results. There are many people, which will not believe in prophetic visions and dreams. They will most likely dispute them and their excuse for this is unbelief in the written Word of God, and what it says about prophecies fulfilled. I say this not to scare anyone or cause panic, but believably this is a warning of what is to come! If

you do not know, but God is forgiving and loving He does not wish that anyone should perish, "*but that all should come to repentance*", read Second Peter 3:9. Therefore, what does God do, *He always warns* us before He executes His wrath. Want proof, He warned the world through Noah for 120 years to build an Ark. He warned Sodom and Gomorrah through Abraham regarding their perverted lifestyle. He sent Jonah who was in the belly of a (great fish) for three days and three nights and then the Lord spoke to the (great fish) and vomited him out to warn the pagan city of Nineveh, and then He sent Nahum to the same city 150 years later.
Recommended Reading: Old Testament
Book of Daniel: Chapters 1 - 12

Would you like to know more?

We Should Pay Attention to Our Dreams - Seven Reasons Too

I am going to quickly share with you why God spoke to various prophets in the Old Testament. I believe it was a means to not only to communicate audibly, but also to reveal His master plans, His will on the canvas of the minds like a movie to the "seers". Those prophets who would carry out and disseminate what he reveals to them. We should pay attention to our dreams, especially the ones that are prophetic because it is God speaking to His chosen, and here are seven reasons too…

The Seven Reasons:

It begins in the Old Testament and sets up a bridge over to the New Testament, and here is how we cross into it.

1. God declares that He would reveal to His prophets first through visions, dreams, and audibly beginning in the Old Testament - [6]*And he said, Hear now my words: If there be a prophet among you, I the LORD will make myself known unto him in a vision, and will speak unto him in a dream.* Numbers 12:6 KJV
2. God grants and provides us with spiritual gifts, and these gifts are supernatural and provided through dreams and declared by Him, just as he did for King Solomon - [5]*In Gibeon the LORD appeared to Solomon in a dream by night: and God said, Ask what I shall give thee.* - [15]*And*

Solomon awoke; and, behold, it was a dream ... First Kings 3:5, 15 KJV

3. The one and only true God did speak through dreams as well, declared in His Word - [10]*I have also spoken by the prophets, and I have multiplied visions, and used similitudes, by the ministry of the prophets*. Hosea 12:10 KJV
4. Did you know that God could provide counsel through dreams? He declares these things in His Word - [7]*I will bless the LORD, who hath given me counsel: my reins also instruct me in the night seasons*. Psalm 16:7 KJV
5. In our dreams, what we see can become things manifested, just as He did with Abraham by declaring a covenant with him - [12]*And when the sun was going down, a deep sleep fell upon Abram; and, lo, an horror of great darkness fell upon him.* [13]*And he said unto Abram, ...* - [18]*In the same day the LORD made a covenant with Abram, saying, Unto thy seed have I given this land, from the river of Egypt unto the great river, the river Euphrates:* Genesis 15:12, 13, 18 KJV
6. Our dreams can cause us to change when it is from God and declared by Him – [14] *For God [does reveal His will; He] speaks not only once, but more than once, even though men do not regard it [including you, Job.].* [15] *[One may hear God's voice] in a dream, in a vision of the night, when deep sleep falls on men while slumbering upon the bed,* [16] *Then He opens the ears of men and seals their instruction [terrifying them with warnings],* [17] *That He may withdraw man from his purpose and cut off pride from him [disgusting him with his own disappointing self-sufficiency].* [18] *He holds him back from the pit [of*

destruction], and his life from perishing by the sword [of God's destructive judgments]. Job 33:14-18 AMP and read the KJV

Now we will cross over the bridge to the New Testament:

7. God communicates through dreams by declaring it - [17]*And it shall come to pass in the last days, saith God, I will pour out of my Spirit upon all flesh: and your sons and your daughters shall prophesy, and your young men shall see visions, and your old men shall dream dreams:* [18]*And on my servants and on my handmaidens I will pour out in those days of my Spirit; and they shall prophesy*: Acts 2:17, 18 KJV – Read Acts 2:16-21

Would you like to know more?

The Prophetic Agenda

The Prophetic Time Clock

The Fulfilling of Prophecy

[CHAPTER 1]

The Dream Occurrence

WHAT I AM about to share with you is what I believe is a true prophetic night vision, and as the title states "The Dream Occurrence." The true prophetic night vision that I am referring to is what most people have heard of, and known as the "rapture" or "caught up". However, as I stated earlier is this, most people will not believe or agree with the writings on the pages of this book, but I am going to share it with you anyway. Well, it started out as a peaceful evening, where nothing took place that was unusual besides prayer and studying the written Word of God. My wife (Rebecca) and I talked for a while about how the written Word of God has the answers to life issues, and if we would just apply it in our daily lives and have the right type of faith we will see the blessings flow. After the discussion, we noticed it was starting to get late, so as my wife and I prepared for lights out for the evening, I kissed her good night and began to fluff up my pillow as I always do. As I vividly remember, I laid my head on the pillow and turned to look at the clock for the last time that evening, it was 11pm on

December 8, 2008. Quickly, I began to close my eyes and drift off to sleep not knowing what was about to be revealed to me, especially in a dream or night vision. I believe the journey began immediately as if time accelerated, and as if God was waiting for me to fall asleep. I say this because in reality, I do not know how long I was asleep before my night vision began. In an instant, transportation to a future event in time occurred. Suddenly, I was lying in the bed next to my wife we were both sitting up in bed. The only things I could view at that time appeared to be in a five-foot radius because the light in the room did not go beyond this radius. You may be asking how was I able to know it was my wife. No, God did not reveal her face to me; but I knew it was my wife because He gave me her hand in marriage and what I was holding was her left hand, and the evidence of the wedding rings that appeared on her middle ring finger. Not only did He reveal the rings on her left hand, I was able to hear and recognize her voice as well. One thing I do believe is that God will show the right amount of proof in order for dissemination of that proof He has revealed out to all that need to know at the appointed place and time, which you will encounter throughout this book. I like to say this a lot, and it is…

Would you like to know more?

Un-forgiveness Or Strife Can Stop Your Flight

Have you ever had a first class ticket to your favorite destination? Have you ever missed a flight? Well, I am here to tell you that you can have a first class ticket, but that does not necessarily mean you will be on that flight. Something can happen to keep you from boarding. As I continue with this night vision, we were still lying in bed talking and one of the things that took place that morning was a disagreement that I was having with my wife that I would not let go. As I continued to make my point, and to prove that I was right, my wife asked me to let it go, but again I did not heed to her request. My wife stated that it is not about who is right or wrong, but what is right. For the second time she said to me, you must let it go so that we can move on. At this point, I was angry, but my wife was not. I did not ask my wife for forgiveness. This is where I did not count the cost for this bad decision or choice. Before continuing, I believe forgiveness is a choice we make through a decision, motivated by obedience to the written Word of God and His command to forgive. The Bible, our (Basic Instructions Before Leaving Earth) manual instructs us to forgive as the Lord forgave us: The written Word of God says… *"Be gentle and forbearing with one another and, if one has a difference (a grievance or complaint) against another, readily pardoning each other; even as the Lord has [freely] forgiven you, so must you also [forgive]."* Colossians 3:13 AMP – Here is a question that can be asked of oneself. How do I forgive someone when I do not feel like doing it? How do we translate our decision to forgive into a change of heart and mind? We forgive *by faith*, out of obedience and love for Jesus Christ and the written Word of God. For a lot of us, Christians and non-Christians forgiveness goes against our sinful nature, we must forgive with (*agape*) love and faith, whether we feel like it or not. We must lean and trust God to do the work in us that is required so that forgiveness will be complete.

As we arose from bed and began to get ourselves ready for the day, not knowing what was about to take place. To us, we believed that it was going to be a normal peaceful day; little did we know that our lives were about to change literally forever and for eternity. Not only was this change going to affect us, but the entire world. Suddenly we were downstairs in our house, we did not eat breakfast or drink coffee, the only thing we began to do is gather our things for the day, and I must say *I still had not asked my wife for forgiveness.* As I clearly remember, I looked at the surroundings and everything appeared to be in place. The living room area was bright because light was coming through the windows, which indicated to me that it was sunny outside. It was a peaceful setting except for what I was still carrying on the inside of me and what was going on between us. As I picked up some books and placed them in my left hand and my wife picked up her purse and other belongings we headed towards the front door. As I opened the door, it was definitely sunny outside, as the evidence of this shined in our living room, and allowing my wife to exit the house first, then I exited the house after her closing the door behind me, locking it, as I would normally do.

Would you like to know more?

Now You See Me, Now You Don't

As we both walked off the porch and down the stairs we were standing on the sidewalk my wife stood about three feet to the right of me. Our house was located near an up-scale downtown area. Before we began to walk to our right, I looked in the direction to my left, downtown; I could see buildings, people, and vehicles moving about. As we started to walk, I was looking at what appeared to be a piece of paper blowing in the street when all of the sudden I heard a loud thunderous *voice*, but I could not quite make it out, and then I heard what sounded like a *trumpet*, and then people screaming very loudly.

> Note: I did know about *"the voice of the archangel, and with the trump of God:"* until I researched in the scriptures. Read First Thessalonians 4:16

I turned my head to my right and my wife had disappeared. "*In a Blink of an Eye*" she was gone! I called out my wife's name Beckie, Beckie! There was no answer from her because she was gone! I immediately knew what was taking place, it was the "*catching away*", she was "*caught up*" right before my very eyes, and I said no God no! I screamed out, why not me! (Remember, *I did not ask my wife for forgiveness nor did I repent*) at that moment, I knew I was not in right standing with God. I immediately asked God for forgiveness, I said to Him that I was sorry, but still I was standing on the street corner still hearing the horrifying screams. Hmm… it dawned on me, it was too late; I just missed my flight, even with a first class ticket reservation; but it was only a reservation. For what appeared to be a split second, I no longer heard the screams, and then all of the sudden I could hear them again. I looked to my left and I could see people running around in chaos and fear, a wheelchair rolling down the street but it was empty, cars running into anything in front of them, but no drivers or anyone in the passenger side. I looked to my right again, and no Beckie. Now my attention is drawn towards a bus to the right of me heading downtown, as I watched it run off the road all the while people are still screaming, and saying what is happening! A lot of people that day did not understand what was going on, but on the other hand their were many who knew what was happening but did not take heed to any forewarnings that may have been disseminated out to them in their past regarding the "rapture" or the "catching away".

They too were part of a large group of unbelievers of Jesus Christ and disobedient to the written Word of God; left behind including me. Your question most likely is why was I (Mark) left behind? The answer to this question is to forewarn and share the experience of the night vision with everyone, and that this can happen to all those that do not line their life up with the written Word of God. Remember, I am an observer and a participant. Do not allow this to happen to you; because I truly believe it will be a time that many lost-souls will not be able to accept or endure what will come forth. I believe I mentioned something similar in this book earlier, but if I did not and you to missed it, here it is again. To counter act not being "left behind" get your life in order with obedience to the written Word of God! Those of you that do not understand this; get your heart, mind, and the spirit of your mind renewed and your overall lifestyle in line the written Word of God.

One of the most interesting parts of this night vision is that no date or time, no clock, no calendar appears to me at any point in time. With this stated, it says in the book of Matthew 24:33 KJV - *So likewise ye, when ye shall see all these things, know that it is near, even at the doors.* You may believe this or not but the signs are indications that Christ is about to return to earth. Truthfully, they refer to the revelation of Christ, and not the rapture. There are obvious signs during the seven-year Tribulation before the revelation, but there are no signs that precede the rapture. However, there are conditions that are prophetically suggesting that the "catching away" event will happen in the near future. It also says in the book of Matthew 24:36 – *But of that day or hour knoweth no man...* So I am not predicting or foretelling a date or time of the "rapture or catching away" but what was revealed to me in this night vision, and that I believe it will happen sooner than we all think, so get *prepared.* The order of events at the time of Christ's coming is clearly stated and understood in the scriptures. The doctrine of the "rapture" or "catching away" of the Church is also stated and understood with clearest expression in the scriptures.

The Rapture Timing Factor

One of the most controversial aspects of the rapture or the catching away is its timing factor. Some place it at the end of the "Tribulation Period", making the rapture or the catching away and Tribulation the same event as tagged as the "Second Coming" as well. Others place it in the middle of the "Tribulation Period". Still others believe that it will occur at the beginning of the "Tribulation Period". The reason for these different viewpoints is that the exact time and revealing of the rapture or the catching away in scripture is not precisely specific, but inferred.

Post-Tribulation Rapture or Catching Away Scriptures:

Some Place the Timing at the end of Tribulation – Let us look at it. It says in the Book of Matthew 24:29 – KJV the Lord portrays His gathering of the saints as an event that will take place "immediately after the tribulation". This suggests that this is a post Tribulation rapture or the catching away. However, keep this in the forefront of your mind that the book of Matthew is pertaining to and written to the Jews to prove that Jesus is the prophesied Messiah or Christ. However, there are many supporting scriptures to backup the prophecies of the rapture.

Mid-Tribulation Rapture or Catching Away Scriptures:

There are a few variations of the Mid-Tribulation "rapture" or the "catching away" concept. The most common is that the Church removal in the exact middle of the Tribulation is when the Antichrist exposure arises. As you look at First Corinthians 15:52, is where this concepts derives which say that the “rapture” or the “catching away” will occur at the blowing of "the last trumpet". The trumpet identifies with the seventh trumpet of the trumpet judgments in the Book of Revelation. Now here it is, since the blowing of the seventh trumpet is in the Book of Revelation Chapter 11, the mid-point of the “Tribulation Period”, one could conclude that the rapture or the catching away occurs in the middle of the “Tribulation Period”. Again, here is the revelation with these two scriptures, and the understanding and interpretation of them. The first is that the last trumpet of First Corinthians 15:52 - is blown for believers whereas the seven trumpet from the Book of Revelation 11:15 is sounded for unbelievers. The Revelation trumpet has no relevance for the Church. The last trumpet of First Corinthians 15:52 is a trumpet for the righteous, calling those to be “caught up” into the clouds. The last trumpet for the unrighteous is the one described in the Book of Revelation 11:15 that the Tribulation is almost at its end.

Pre-Wrath Rapture or Catching Away Scriptures:

When you look at the pre-wrath “rapture” or the “catching away”, the relationship to the mid-tribulation rapture or the catching away concept arises. It places it at the beginning of the last quarter of the “Tribulation Period”, or about five and a half years into the Tribulation. Read about the bowl judgments in the Book of Revelation Chapter 6 where Jesus Himself breaks the seals, Chapter 8 initiates the trumpet judgments and is given their trumpets at the throne of God, and Chapter 16 the last quarter of the Tribulation represent the wrath of God. Read these chapters in order to obtain understanding and revelation in the Spirit of God.

Pre-Tribulation Rapture or Catching Away Scriptures:

I believe the best conclusion of the scripture is that the "rapture" or the "catching away" will occur at the beginning of the or right before the "Tribulation Period". The most important reason I believe this has to do with imminence (impending warning, danger) of what is going to happen. Repeatedly in scripture, it says to watch for the appearing of the Lord. It says… "Watch therefore": Matthew 24:42, "*Therefore be ye also ready*" Matthew 24:44, "to be on the alert", and "to be dressed in readiness". It says in Luke 12:35 "*and your lights burning*". Take heed to these persistent warnings because Jesus can appear at any moment. These prophetic events shall happen first before the appearance of the Lord. There are numerous scriptures to backup the catching away and especially end-time prophecies. Nevertheless, I also know that there are many, which do not believe in the rapture or the catching away, or the end-times. That is why God provided us a free will, as a (free morale agent) to make decisions and choices. He does not force us to believe in Him or His son Jesus Christ.

Key Reference Scriptures:

[1] The vision of Isaiah the son of Amoz, which he saw concerning Judah and Jerusalem in the days of Uzziah, Jotham, Ahaz, and Hezekiah, kings of Judah.
Isaiah 1:1 KJV

The key scriptures in Acts 2 is verse 17 and 18
[16] But this is that which was spoken by the prophet Joel;
[17] And it shall come to pass in the last days, saith God, I will pour out of my Spirit upon all flesh: and your sons and your daughters shall prophesy, and your young men shall see visions, and your old men shall dream dreams:
[18] And on my servants and on my handmaidens I will pour out in those days of my Spirit; and they shall prophesy:
Acts 2:16-18 KJV

[51] Take notice! I tell you a mystery (a secret truth, an event decreed by the hidden purpose or counsel of God). We shall not all fall asleep [in death], but we shall all be changed (transformed)
[52] In a moment, in the twinkling of an eye, at the [sound of the] last trumpet call. For a trumpet will sound, and the dead [in Christ] will be raised imperishable (free and immune from decay), and we shall be changed (transformed).
First Corinthians 15:51, 52 AMP – Note: Read the King James Version as well

The key scripture in First Thessalonians 4 is verse 17

13 But I would not have you to be ignorant, brethren,
concerning them which are asleep, that ye sorrow not, even as
others which have no hope.
14 For ij we believe that Jesus died and rose again, even so
them also which sleep in Jesus will God bring with him.
15 For this we say unto you by the word oj the Lord, that we
which are alive and remain unto the coming oj the Lord shall
not prevent them which are asleep.
16 For the Lord himself shall descend from heaven with a shout,
with the voice of the archangel, and with the trump of God:
and the dead in Christ shall rise first:
17 Then we which are alive and remain shall be caught up
together with them in the clouds, to meet the Lord in the air:
and so shall we ever be with the Lord.

First Thessalonians 4:13-17 KJV: Follow up with Second Thessalonians 2:1 KJV

A Whole Truth Nugget:

You must get the whole truth of the written Word of God, not a partial truth. Read and study these scriptures and all the scriptures so that you get a clear understanding and revelation of the written Word of God. There are some in various religious groups and in non-religious groups, which believe God does not speak to true men and women of God through visions and dreams anymore. Well, I beg to differ. The few that are not getting full understanding and revelation say that this only took place with the prophets in the Old Testament, but the scriptures clearly states that He (God) does in the New Testament as well. Another way that He (God) speaks to us is through the written Word of God.

Would you like to know more?

[CHAPTER 2] Undercover Teaching

WITH ALL OF THE CHAOS that was taking place around me, I believe that God wanted me to see enough with clarity and proof of what it will be like when the rapture takes place. I believe that He wants me to tell the people the truth, warn them that this shall happen. I believe that He assigned this to me because of the type of details that is required to come forth, and that God continues to reveal things to His true prophets first, just as He revealed to the prophet Isaiah and Daniel. So as I continue with this night vision, all of the sudden I was no longer standing in front of our house or observing what was taking place in the downtown area, but in an instant I was immediately transported to a location that appeared to be a gymnasium. It was dark, but enough light that I could see what was necessary for me to see. I was sitting on a bleacher, third row with other people but surrounded by a number of men on the first two rows to the right of me and to the left of me, and off in the distance I could see a doorway where light was shining through it. Sitting on my right was a dark skinned figure of a man; I could see the left side of his face, which also displayed the outline of his beard going down the left side of his face. One of the things I attempted to do is look directly into his face, but I was not able to accomplish this. I believe it was not for me to look directly into his face, but only see what God was allowing me see. Now here is what I could not understand, I was able to make out what he was wearing. He was wearing a brown leather jacket and a checkered colored shirt, and again I attempted to look into his face, but again access denied. I believe it was not for me to know who was sitting next to me and left behind because if I knew, it would cause major issues for that person and me. In other words, if I knew who was sitting next to me could indicate that I will not be "caught up" along with the man sitting next to me. Again, I must continue to reiterate this, I am an observer and a participant.

As I continued to look around, I was not able to look into anyone's face at all as much as I attempted to. While sitting there, in front of me stood, what appeared to be a tall figure of a man, his body outlined in the light shining through the door in the distance, he was wearing dark clothing, and in his hand appeared to be a Bible, but I could not clearly see it! Is it possible that this man was preparing to preach the word and read scriptures even though the Body of Christ was "caught up" in the clouds?

> Read: [3]Saying, Hurt not the earth, neither the sea, nor the trees, *till we have sealed the servants of our God in their foreheads.*
>
> [4]And I heard the number of them which were sealed: and there were sealed an hundred and forty and four thousand of all the tribes of the children of Israel.
>
> Revelation 7:3, 4 KJV
>
> The 144,000 of all the tribes of the children of Israel saved first.

Is it possible that this man was about to bring forth the Word of God to all the people that was in that gymnasium? If so, it is apparent, we had to hide in order to get any type of teaching and preaching of the written Word of God after the rapture or caught up event. I believe many people will experience a conversion (still saved by grace and mercy during the tribulation time) and become followers of Jesus Christ. However, it will be challenging! After this, new born again believers of Jesus Christ will be hunted down, many killed by numerous followers of the "*man of sin*" the *Antichrist*. Now I understand why the title of Chapter 2 is (Undercover Teaching). Those that remain will experience extreme difficulty to openly read the written Word of God from the Bible or openly hear a sermon coming from a Preacher, Minister, Pastor, or anyone that has knowledge of the written Word of God. However, do not fret, there are some spiritual solutions regarding the preaching of the written Word of God, as I will explain shortly. Now this will not take place immediately, but will eventually take place shortly after the rapture or the caught up. To continue, as this man, a possible Minister of the Gospel began to bring forth the written Word of God, I attempted to look into his face, but it was not available to view. Then he began speaking to a man on the right of me sitting on the second row, after he was done with him, he asked the man if he had preached the written Word of God last week, and he nodded his head yes in agreement. However, nothing else followed behind that question. There is evidence here that the man who nodded his head yes to the question was a Preacher, Minister, etc. or someone who possibly was self-appointed and not chosen by God to teach and preach the written Word of God. False teaching and false prophets is more prevalent today than ever before, because the evidence of this is taking place now. The Bible mentions this very clearly. Humanity will experience this after the rapture or the caught up as well. I do believe that his lifestyle did not line up with the written Word of God. If this were not the case, he would not have been sitting on those bleachers, left behind. Rest assured that men and women in this position will not be "caught up" in the clouds on that first class flight to heaven. As this night vision continues, I could only hear a few words or sentences, not everything was for me to know. I was puzzled at times in how all this was taking place around me. If I could just look into someone's face. I really wanted to identify with someone, anyone.

It appeared and felt that I was all alone in a world of disobedient "left behinds". In my mind, as far as I knew, the people I was familiar with were gone, including my wife. I must say, that one of the most interesting things taking place is that my five physical senses (smelling, seeing, hearing, tasting, and touching) in this night vision are still enabled and active. Wow!

Physical senses become spiritual senses operating in the night vision in the prophetic dream realm. What am I to do? Well, I knew I must repent and be one hundred percent faithful, sold-out for God and ask for forgiveness! However, I also believe that it was for me to view the future, record the future, report back to the Body of Christ, including the world, and share it with everyone that would believe it and receive it. I stated earlier in this chapter that there are some spiritual solutions of what a person can do in order for Jesus Christ to be Lord and savior in their life if left behind. I want to share with everyone and disseminate four avenues of how the lost is reached during the “Tribulation Period”. Take note that this takes place after the rapture, or the “caught up” of the Church.

Would you like to know more?

Four Avenues to Reach the Lost During the Tribulation Period

In order to reach the lost during the "Tribulation Period" the written Word of God contains the answers and the instructions on what to do, and pay attention to. The Bible says that a great multitude of people will accept Jesus Christ as Lord and savior in their lives during this time. It is very interesting how God still loves and cares about the people left behind. He still wants to give them another opportunity to get it right.

How God Will Reach The Lost:

1. God's Two Witnesses – The Book of Revelation speaks about two witnesses, two prophets risen from the dead that will bust on the scene during the first half (3 ½ years) of the Tribulation. God will give them supernatural power to prophesy, dispense astonishing miracles, and *witness* to the grace of God. They will produce an enormous soul harvest of the first forty-two months or 1260 days of the Tribulation, and will warn Israel and the world, at the temple site, that the coming judgment is about to fall upon the world. In addition to this, they will attempt to call Israel to repentance by proclaiming the gospel, and urge her to accept her Messiah.
Read the Book of Revelation 11:3-13 KJV

2. The 144,000 Jewish Servants of God – Also during the first half (3 ½ years) of the Tribulation period God is going to mark in their foreheads with His seal. These 144,000 servants are Evangelists they come from the 12 tribes of Israel, 12,000 from each. They are

the first set of Jews saved and accept Jesus Christ as their true Messiah, and they play a major role in the multitude that is converted to Christians. God endows them with the anointing, protection and power from on high. God will use them to do the following: 1) *the proclamation of the everlasting gospel*, 2) *the fall of Babylon,* 3) *the judgment of the lost, and* 4) *the blessedness of the saved.* Please pay attention to number one. The Gospel preached to the lost! Read Revelation 14:1-5 KJV – Now God is about to for the first time in history send angels to proclaim to all the people on earth that personal faith in Jesus death and resurrection can save them.
Read the Book of Revelation 7:1-4 and 9-14 and Revelation 14:1-5 KJV

3. God Sends an Angel of The Everlasting Gospel – Now here is where God will make an exception during this period by sending *an angel* to preach and witness to the people on earth in a supernatural manner before the end comes. It says in Revelation 14:6 "[6]*And I saw another angel fly in the midst of heaven,*" – This angel will preach too "*every race and tribe and language and people.*" I believe God shall send more than one angel to perform different tasks on the earth. This angel will preach at the "*for the hour of his judgment is come*" At this point-in-time, I believe things are about to end.
Read the Book of Revelation 14:6, 7 KJV

4. An Outpouring of the Holy Spirit – In the latter days it will be very prevalent that God will pour out His Holy Spirit upon the flesh on humanity throughout the earth. Read Joel 2:28-32 KJV and Acts 2:17, 18. It is imperative that one is able to hear God's voice in a supernatural manner during this troubling period. In the

Old Testament thousands of years ago, called "the time of Jacob's trouble" and in the New Testament labeled as "the time of Gentiles trouble" but the word says … "*but he will be saved out of it*" Jeremiah 30:7. Your relationship with God is very important! The reason why I say this is because as mentioned earlier in this chapter. Many Christians shall experience a horrible death because of their faith in Jesus Christ during the "Tribulation Period". The name for this is Martyrdom.
Read the Book of Joel 2:28-32 KJV

Now that the four avenues of how the lost is reached during the "Tribulation Period", what will you do if left behind? I say this to all that is reading this book at this point-in-time. Do not wait after the rapture to become a born again believer of Jesus Christ. If you have not accepted Jesus Christ as your Lord and Savior in your life, I highly recommend you do it now. Do it before the rapture or the caught up. Do it right now! Obtain understanding of your conversion, repent (heart/mind change), have faith, continue to pray daily, and have forgiveness in your heart, by obeying, which is the major key to the written Word of God. It really does take all this and more! Do not believe those that tell you that it does not take all of this to be in right standing with God because those that say this are truly deceived. In other words, do not allow deception to form in your mind, heart or the spirit of your mind by wrong teachings and doctrines. It is imperative that one gird up (protect) his (heart and mind) and protect his (ear-gate and eye-gate), and continue to *renew your mind* (Romans 12:1, 2) and the *spirit of your mind* (Ephesians 4:23) with the written Word of God.

Time Is Running Out For Humanity

The truth of the matter is that time is truly running out for all humanity. Our lease on this earth is about to end, and a new permanent leasing agreement will be signed. Many will not have an opportunity to sign the new lease because of permanent eviction from the new earth and new heaven that will come forth. However, when people put their heads in the sand or in the clouds, they do not want to know the truth. Rejection of Jesus Christ and the Word of God is more prevalent today than ever before. This has been an issue for nearly (6,000 plus) years of man's rule. The plus is the extra (thousand years). The Lord thy God has a prophetic agenda or master plan. It consists of this… I believe the Lord thy God implemented His 7,000-year master plan, by the seven-day week. Genesis 1:3-31 shows us that God created the earth in six days and then created the seventh-day Sabbath by resting on it as you read this in Genesis 2:2, 3. Therefore, here is God allowing man to work six days, which I believe is (six thousand years), and followed with the seventh day to rest or a (1,000-year Sabbath rest).

The Apostle Peter wrote, "*…that one day is with the Lord as a thousand years, and a thousand years as one day.*" (2nd Peter 3:8). No doubt, he understood that the seven-day week pictured the 7,000-year prophetic agenda of God. The Apostle Paul also had on his mental that when he instructed that the seventh day of the week pictures the millennial rule of Christ that will follow this present evil age of human misrule on earth as written in (Hebrews 4:3-11). This day will "come to pass" after Christ's intervention and it will last a thousand years (Revelation 20:1-4). You can reference this principle by reading Psalm 90:4 and Hosea 6:2. As you obtain revelation of the seventh day of the week, it symbolizes the 1,000-year ruler ship of Jesus Christ; thus, the first six days of the week picture 6,000-years of man governing himself to work out his own ideas and plans. I believe each day of the week represents a 1,000-year period according to the covenant Word of God.

Not knowing the truth, understanding, and revelation of the written Word of God is one of the biggest issues along with disobedience, and having the right type of faith (belief) in what the Word of God says. Because of this, judgment shall happen "*come to pass*". So what is the truth? I believe this night vision is the truth of what is to come because the Word of God says in Amos 3:7 – *"Surely the Lord GOD will do nothing, but he reveals his secret to his servants the prophets"*. So what is the truth? The truth is the (Basic Instructions Before Leaving Earth) manual, the Bible, the written Word of God. So diligently seek (search or research) Him, and one will discover that true prophecy revealed is unfolding before ones very eyes. Can you see it? One can believe this or not, but time is running out for humanity and I truly believe that we will see and witness the end of this age. Prepare yourself and take hold of this prophetic night vision, and believe it! Just as God gave Noah instructions to build a great ship, tagged "Noah's Ark", and that He (God) would bring forth a great flood to the earth because of man's disobedience. Noah attempted to warn the people, but they laughed at him, mocked God, and the only believers was his immediate family. Do not be like this group of unbelievers, but believe it! As this chapter ends, and another chapter of the night vision begins, remember this… "[29]*And now I have told you before it come to pass, that, when it is come to pass, ye might believe*". John 14:29 KJV

Would you like to know more?

[CHAPTER 3]
God's GPS Effect

AS MY NIGHT VISION journey continues, it was apparent that it was time for me to move on from the previous scene and location because God revealed to me what He wanted me to see in the previous chapter. Therefore, in an instant, He transports me to another location, an outside setting. I thought it was an unusual place for me to be, because it was familiar to me. I said to myself, I have been here before. It was a park, Carver Park from my childhood days, which still exist today. This made no sense to me, why would God send me to a place of familiarity. I believe that it does not matter where you are or from, it will be a worldwide event. According to God, he placed me in the right place for the right time. It is interesting how (God's Positioning System) is extremely accurate; because He would never lead anyone down the wrong path, provide a wrong turn or location … It says in Psalm 139:7-10 AMP

> *[7] Where could I go from Your Spirit? Or where could I flee*
> *from Your presence? [8]If I ascend up into heaven, You are*
> *there; if I make my bed in Sheol (the place of the dead),*
> *behold, You are there. [9]If I take the wings of the morning or*
> *dwell in the uttermost parts of the sea, [10]Even there shall*
> *Your hand lead me, and Your right hand shall hold me.*

His presence is "omnipresence" which means being present everywhere at the same time. The attributes of God are divine as He is everywhere at the same time. God's presence is continuous throughout all of creation of earth and heaven, though not revealed in the same way at the same time to people everywhere. At times, He may be actively present in a situation or location while He may not reveal that He is present in another circumstance in some other area. However, I believe He was there, observing me, listening to the conversation by people He placed there, and my responses. One cannot exclude God from any location. He is the one that is taking me on this journey, so that dissemination to all people of this earth is accomplished. As this night vision continues, it was a sunny day as I stood next to a green electrical transformer, holding a mobile phone in my hand but talking to no one. Why did I have this mobile phone in my hand? Was God going to allow me to contact someone or warn someone, at this point in time I do not know? While standing there, I could see various color clothing that people are wearing while they walked around in the park, but I could not look directly into their eyes or recognize anyone's face. They were just wondering around as if they were lost or in a daze. On the other side of the electrical transformer to my left stands a man just observing focused on looking straight ahead, not saying anything to me or to anyone else. One may be asking how I knew it was a man. It was his stature. I looked at the right side of his face and it was just a grey outline! All of the sudden, he began to talk to me, but I could not understand a word he was saying. It made no sense to me, why is it that I can hear the sound of his voice but not understand any of the words he was speaking? Could it be that if I could understand what he was saying, that I would recognize him by his voice? My God, my God, He really wants this secret protected, and for now kept from his prophet. I am calling this His (divine protection mechanism) to protect me, and others and the integrity of the Bible's prophecies. It is apparent that no matter where God transports me in time, He is not allowing me to recognize anyone left behind. As stated earlier, my wife was an exception when it came to identifying her as "caught up" into the air with the Lord.

The man that was talking to me all of the sudden stopped talking. I could not think of any apparent reason why, but he did. Only God knows for sure. At this time I was looking down at the ground still in somewhat of a daze myself. I looked up, stepped forward, and turned to my left. I thought that I recognized someone; finally, what I thought would be a familiar face. As this tall figure approached me, he was tall and instead of a grey face, he had a white face. Why a white face? What could this mean? Is there a significant difference between a grey face compared to a white face? Is it possible that the grey faces are demonic (the enemy) and the white faces are angels (spiritual/angelic/friendly)? As he draws nearer to me, he was wearing a white shirt and light brown khaki pants. As I began to walk towards him, he stops in his tracks, and I stop as well. For some reason, neither one of us could advance towards each other any further. The distance between us was roughly 40 feet. As I began to speak to him, I asked him this question, hey I need the phone number to, uh, uh (oh wow, I could not pronounce the name of the person or persons to call)! Then I followed up with, I need to call some friends and family at home, work and warn them of what is about to take place. His response was, you cannot call anyone or warn anyone of anything. My response to him, is why not? I have a mobile phone! Again, my statement to him, I have a mobile phone! After making the statement he turns and begins to walk away, my question never answered regarding the asking for the phone numbers. This makes no sense to me! As he walks farther and farther away, I can see him fade away, and vanishes in the distance. So where did he go? Why was he there to say, (you cannot call anyone or warn anyone of anything). I stood there not knowing what to say. Was he a messenger to warn me of something, or just inform me that I cannot warn anyone of what is to come? Nevertheless, I said I must tell others! As I turned around and headed back to the green electrical transformer because this was a familiar landmark for me but as I approached it the man that was standing there from the beginning, is now gone. So where did this man go? Did he fulfill his assignment? I believe both men did. Yes, this is a night vision but some things that would be normal in the natural (like calling people to warn), but in this night vision (dream) dimension it is different; depending on the situation at hand it may not be allowed.

Here is something that we all must give thought to, because of where we are right now at this appointed time, especially with new technology? One question you must ask yourself, and it is will the mobile network have monitoring protocols in place. I say yes! With today's mobile and smart-phone technology we have GPS location enabled devices, RFID (Radio Frequency Identification) tracking, and other services already in place. I believe that the (Antichrist) will control and/or use various media outlets, such as the press, social media, and communication channels to televise and promote his agenda. We see evidence of these things orchestrated and put in place now as this book comes into fruition, and as I share this night vision. As one examines there relationship with God, it is vital that one knows that we are living in perilous times and that it is imperative that one is saved by accepting Jesus Christ as Lord and Savoir. Remember, there is only one-way unto the Father (John 14:6 KJV), and to enter into the Kingdom of God. Do not allow deception by new age religion that there is more than one-way. I say this, before I continue with this night vision, I want to take you on a slight detour in the next chapter of prophetic signs, and it starts now…

[CHAPTER 4]

Prophetic Signs Can You See It

YES! THIS IS A TRUE night vision regarding the "catching away". However, we really must be aware of additional things in conjunction to the rapture or the catching away; some of these things will be before, during or after the rapture or the catching away. Oh, we must not leave out the Tribulation period. Can you see it? Can you see the prophetic signs? They are right in front of you. Can you see it? The Bible provides many true prophetic signs that warn us of the coming end of the age, and it is very much apparent in the earth. What did Jesus Christ prophesy? Well, Jesus Christ prophesied about false prophets, false teachers, (Matthew 24:5, 11) rumors of wars, famines, earthquakes, tribulations, and the Gospel preached throughout the world (mention earlier), we see that this is already happening. Can you see it? Right now, it is very important that all of humanity should prepare for what is coming in the very near future; but many will not take heed to this preparation because they do not believe in Jesus Christ as their Savior, and they do not believe in what the Bible prophesises. I say this, failure to address sin; unbelief in God or Jesus Christ and these matters by passively ignoring the realities around us will not prevent what will happen. The writing in this book is to get your attention, to wake you up, to teach you what is true as a prophetic night vision. When God brings forth something prophetic such as a word of prophecy, a gift of prophecy or the spirit of prophecy it needs to come forth to not only warn the people, but also encourage the people to take authentic positive action on these instructions and directions with the right heart and mindset. Everything that I share with you is for this appointed time such as now, and is relevant now and until Jesus Christ returns to this earth for His Church. I say again can you see it? Can you see the prophetic signs? Now, let us examine the text further in Matthew 24:15, 16 because here it is right here…

> 15 When ye therefore shall see the abomination of desolation, spoken of by Daniel the prophet, stand in the holy place, (whoso readeth, let him understand:)
> 16 Then let them which be in Judea flee into the mountains:
> …

Now, the first thing you must pay attention to is (the abomination of desolation). Now the prophet Daniel spoke of this in (Daniel 9:27). This abomination of desolation will "come to pass" on the Temple Mount. What this entails is that the Temple Mount in Jerusalem; an attempt to place it under a sharing arrangement between Jew and Gentile, and we see this written in (Revelation 11:1-2) where it talks about the rebuilding of the temple or more likely the prophesied millennial temple. However, this agreement will not workout. This statement right here is what will (wet your noodle). Earlier in this paragraph, it is mention that a sharing arrangement between Jew and Gentile be made. If you go back to the year 2000 this sharing arrangement suggestion actually made by our former President, Bill Clinton in July of that year. Hmm, the President at that time had no idea what he was saying. Based on that statement, he (President Clinton) believed that this is the only possible solution to the Temple Mount dispute but unfortunately, it is not. Would you like to know how this actually came about? If so, those of us who were paying attention to this can discern where we are right now in biblical prophecy.

Quote:

> "Ariel Sharon (2000), Camp David, 11 July 2000 - Israeli and Palestinian delegations meet to hold peace talks under American sponsorship. Israeli Prime Minister, Ehud Barak, tells US President, Bill Clinton, his starting position: Jerusalem would never be shared. Palestinian Chairman, Yasser Arafat, demands half Jerusalem as his capital and Palestinian sovereignty over what the Muslims know as the Haram al-Sharif, which is the Jews' Temple Mount. The Americans draft an agreement and first present it to Barak. The draft appears to allow the Palestinians also to have their capital in Jerusalem. Barak angrily rejects it, so an amendment is added to the agreement, to take account of Israel's position. Then the paper is presented to Arafat. He notices the amended paragraph which addresses the subject of

sovereignty over Jerusalem, and he too angrily rejects the paper, stating that the most important thing for him is Jerusalem and the Haram al-Sharif (Temple Mount). The Americans try to bridge the gap, but for a whole week every American effort is rejected by one side or the other and Barak, who had made all the running for this summit, now refuses pointblank to negotiate directly with Arafat. President Clinton, who is due to leave for the G8 summit in Japan the next day, finally confronts Ehud Barak and tells him that he has got to make a better offer. Barak consults his negotiating team and they all agree that some sacrifice over Jerusalem must be made in order to avoid an eruption of violence. Barak, however, is well aware that to do so could be political suicide. They argue all day long while Clinton waits and waits and getting more and more angry. Late at night, Barak arrives at Clinton's cabin with his offer: a couple of Palestinian villages on the outskirts of Jerusalem could become their capital. He stresses the point that no Israeli Prime Minister would ever give up sovereignty over Temple Mount. President Clinton explodes and very angrily says to Barak, 'You made me wait here for thirteen hours and you come back with this? You go say it to Arafat if you want to. Don't ask me to do it. I'm not going to do that. You dragged me to Geneva for a summit with Assad. I was your puppet! And then you backed off! I will not let it happen here again. You got to go further, you got to be able to see enough in your proposal to believe that if they give and you give and they give and you give they'll get some place they can live with. You've got to do better. You have got to do better.' Barak goes back to his cabin. Then, he decides to break a taboo and makes a huge concession. When he returns to Clinton, he says, 'I am willing for you to propose to Arafat that we divide the Old City between us.' Barak says to Clinton that he is willing to offer the Palestinians East Jerusalem as a capital and sovereignty over the Muslim and the Christian quarters in the Old City. Barak argues that if Arafat does not accept this offer, it would prove that he is using terrorism not just as a tactic in negotiations but as a way of life. He then asks Clinton to present his proposal to the Palestinian leader as an American idea. President Clinton calls Arafat to his cabin and presents him the deal. But one part of the package is totally rejected by Arafat. When it comes to Haram al-Sharif (Temple Mount), the holy place in the Old City that matters most to Arafat, Barak still insists that Israel retain sovereignty here. Arafat would get only custodianship. Now Arafat is under pressure. Clinton reprimands him for not moving an inch from his starting position. He tells him that if he turns down the offer, he would lose the relationship with the United States and everything would be off the table. Arafat has to be in defense. He takes the President's hand and says, 'You're my only friend, I can't afford to lose you.' He then returns to his cabin to consult with his team. Arafat is of the opinion that he cannot be flexible in regards to Arabic and Muslim issues, otherwise he would be assassinated, and stresses that the main issue is the Holy City places. Arafat's answer to Clinton is that he cannot betray Jerusalem, which means 'No.' President Clinton delays his departure for Japan to talk Arafat round, in vain. But then he tries a calculated fudge on Barak. He relays to Barak his conversation with Arafat, exaggerating what Arafat had said, and then he leaves for Okinawa for the G8 Summit. The Israeli and Palestinian delegations stay behind in Camp David. Barak, as a result of what Clinton told him, is under the impression that Arafat had actually agreed to negotiate on the basis his offer. Arafat, on the other hand, is left with the impression that negotiations would continue without reference to what had been put on the table. The next morning Barak finds out that Arafat hadn't agreed to his terms at all and he is very angry. He refuses to meet Arafat one on one. When Clinton returns to Camp David, he finds that both sides still cling to their positions: Barak would not yield the sovereignty over Temple Mount or Haram and Arafat wouldn't accept the settlement without it".

If this does not (wet your noodle) then I do not know what will! If the former President, Bill Clinton only knew, what he was saying at that point and time. However, when you examine ignorance, it does equal (not knowing.) Here it is again, prophecy unfolding right before our very ears and eyes. Can you see it? Can you see prophecy fulfilled?

Now, the second thing you must pay attention to is (*Then let them which be in Judea flee into the mountains*: ...). Two major events out of many will take place three and one-half years before the Battle of Armageddon. One is the halting of the sacrifices at the temple in Jerusalem, and the second event is the invasion and occupation of Israel by an alliance of nations and Israel's Islamic neighbors. As stated, (*Then let them which be in Judea flee into the mountains*: ... Matthew 24:16) and *...For then shall be great tribulation, such as was not since the beginning of the world to this time, no, nor ever shall be* - Matthew 24:21. These things shall "come to pass" at the appointed time and I truly believe that the (world stage is being set for it right now!)

Jesus said to us concerning these events:

> *"...when ye shall see all these things, know that it is near, even at the doors. Verily I say unto you, This generation shall not pass, till all these things be fulfilled."* Matthew 24:33, 34.

Now what I am about to share with you at this time will be a worldwide event viewed in real-time spiritually and in the natural framework in the earth. Before I continue with this dream and night vision, I want to direct your attention to the following…

Two Insights from the Apostle Paul - Prophesied Apostasy

The First Insight:

1. The great falling away from Faith: It says… –
   [3]*Let no man deceive you by any means: for that day shall not come, except there come a falling away first, and that man of sin be revealed, the son of perdition;* [4]*Who opposeth and exalteth himself above all that is called God, or that is worshipped; so that he as God sitteth in the temple of God, shewing himself that he is God.*
   Second Thessalonians 2:3, 4 KJV

   In verse 3: The word apostasy means "a standing away from" in the sense of "falling away – Gr. *apostasia*", withdrawal, or defection from the truth of the Word of God. There are those in every generation who fall away, but this is a general condition prior to the revelation of the Antichrist.
   In verse 4: Sitteth in the Temple of God – When the Antichrist desecrates the rebuilt Temple of Jerusalem.

   [1]*Now the Spirit speaketh expressly, that in the latter times some shall depart from the faith, giving heed to seducing spirits, and doctrines of devils;* [2]*Speaking lies in hypocrisy; having their conscience seared with a hot iron;* [3]*Forbidding to marry, and commanding to abstain*

> *from meats, which God hath created to be received with thanksgiving of them which believe and know the truth.*
> First Timothy 4:1-3 KJV
>
> In verse 1: We see the word (**expressly** – which means clearly). To (**depart** – interpreted as to apostatize). In other words, we see that apostasy is the deliberate and permanent rejection of Christianity after a previous profession of faith. *This is that falling away effect.* At the end of the verse, we see (**Doctrines of devils** – interpreted as doctrines taught by demonic spirits).
>
> In verse 2: The interpretation here is the (**"hypocrisy of liars"**): When looking back at verse 1 the expounding of doctrines, not directly, but indirectly through human ministers influenced by internal demonic spirits and by external demonic influence. Now read (**having their conscience seared with a hot iron**), branded or scarred in their mental (conscience or mind). They lead a life of hypocrisy, yet continue to preach to others.
>
> In verse 3: As you read and understand this verse, two true examples of demonic doctrines reveal itself. The prohibition against marriage is cited and abstaining from certain foods.

Many religions are embracing the new age interfaith agenda, and denying Jesus Christ as the only way to the (Father) and eternal salvation. What we are seeing today is an ever-increasing politically correct media, a more corrupt society, the embracing of homosexuality, and lesbianism as an acceptable alternate lifestyle, environmentalist movement (worship of mother earth), reincarnation, karma, and belief in past lives that contradicts the Word of God. I must not leave this one out; there are those that are very critical to all who would eat the meat God provides us as nourishment for our physical bodies. When it comes to teaching and preaching the truth of the written Word of God compromise dominates, especially when it comes to true eternal salvation for this world.

The Second Insight:

2. The Godlessness Generation Y: It says in… -
   [1] *This know also, that in the last days perilous times shall come.* [2] *For men shall be lovers of their own selves, covetous, boasters, proud, blasphemers, disobedient to parents, unthankful, unholy,* [3] *Without natural affection, trucebreakers, false accusers, incontinent, fierce, despisers of those that are good,* [4] *Traitors, heady, highminded, lovers of pleasures more than lovers of God;* [5] *Having a form of godliness, but denying the power thereof: from such turn away.*
   Second Timothy 3:1-5 KJV

   In verses 1-4: In (**the last days**), it really begins with the birth of Jesus Christ and His return to this earth to establish His kingdom. Prophecy regarding (perilous times) is an indication of (**the coming apostasy**) characterizes the final days of the Church age. Can you see it?

   In verse 5: (**A form of godliness**), means a mere religion without (**power**) or spiritual life. Paul said this to Timothy to turn away from this. This still applies today.

It is prevalent that false teachers and teaching is alive and well.

As we look at how things have summed up the following. We see corporate greed, financial corruption on Wall Street, and the continued downturn of the economy it is apparent that the signs point to end-time prophecy fulfilled right now. One prevalent sign is the New Age Movement of mystics, and spiritual gurus who claim to be the enlightened ones. They are educated and influential but they lack the truth of the written Word of God.

Biblical Prophecies - Alignment for the End of the Age

Now let us begin by aligning various prophetic dreams, visions, and the prophetic Word of God and the fulfilling of Bible prophecy, and what took place in the past and what will "come to pass" as now time prophecy, and as prophesied future events. These biblical prophecies are specific and in order according to the scriptures, and to wake one up to what is to come in the very near future.

A Few Biblical Prophecies:

First, we must divide the Book of Revelation up into three parts…
Past: The "things which" you have seen…
Present: The "things which" are…
Future: The "things which" shall be hereafter...

1. The Prophecy - The book of Revelation (which means, the unveiling of something previously unrevealed) indicates that a two hundred million man cavalry will one day come out of the east first, and then the northern parts of Israel. Who is this cavalry or army?

Scripture:

[16]*And the number of the army of the horsemen were two hundred thousand thousand: and I heard the number of them.* Revelation 9:16 KJV

The Apostle John heard the number of the Horsemen: 200,000,000 – literally, "two myriads of myriads". John who was an Apostle, ended up on the island of Patmos because the Roman emperor Domitian about A.D. 95 exiled him there. John the Apostle saw his visions, and told to write them down while he was on the island of Patmos.

2. The Prophecy - The rebuilding of the Roman Empire as a (European Union) shall continue to evolve and come forth. Currently there are 27 states and counting…

Scripture:

> [32] *This image's head was of fine gold, his breast and his arms of silver, his belly and his thighs of brass,* [33]*His legs of iron, his feet part of iron and part of clay.* Daniel 2:32, 33 KJV

> [40] *And the fourth kingdom shall be strong as iron: forasmuch as iron breaketh in pieces and subdueth all things: and as iron that breaketh all these, shall it break in pieces and bruise.*
> [41]*And whereas thou sawest the feet and toes, part of potters' clay, and part of iron, the kingdom shall be divided; but there shall be in it of the strength of the iron, forasmuch as thou sawest the iron mixed with miry clay.* [42]*And as the toes of the feet were part of iron, and part of clay, so the kingdom shall be partly strong, and partly broken.* [43]*And whereas thou sawest iron mixed with miry clay, they shall mingle themselves with the seed of men: but they shall not cleave one to another, even as iron is not mixed with clay.* Daniel 2:40-43 KJV

According to Daniel's interpretation of the dream that King Nebuchadnezzar had, the fourth kingdom of iron represents the Roman Empire. The two legs represent the division of the Roman Empire. The European nations and the Roman Empire are still currently separate.

3. The Prophecy - The rebuilding or reconstruction of the Temple in Jerusalem -

Scripture:

> [7]*And I will shake all nations, and the desire of all nations shall come: and I will fill this house with glory, saith the LORD of hosts.* Haggai 2:7 KJV

The prophet Haggai speaks of a temple situated upon the site of previous temples. This scripture refers to as *this house* – at the time of Christ's return. There are many groups already working on preparations for the building of a new temple. This new temple is the Third Temple of Jerusalem on the Temple Mount. Yes, the blueprints are completed, the temple garments made, and attempts to lay the cornerstone of the temple. One thing stands in the way of the reconstruction of the new temple, and it is Islam's third holiest site, which is the Dome of the Rock and government support.

> [1]*And there was given me a reed like unto a rod: and the angel stood, saying, Rise, and measure the temple of God, and the altar, and them that worship therein.*
> [2]*But the court which is without the temple leave out, and measure it not; for it is given unto the Gentiles: and the holy city shall they tread under foot forty and two months.*
> Revelation 11:1, 2 KJV

In the Book of Revelation 11:2 this is prophesied as an end-time prophecy and is expected to take place during the Tribulation period or (more likely) the prophesied millennial temple shall "come to pass" as a future event on the earth.

Side Note: Read Second Thessalonians 2:4 KJV – In verse-4 (Sitteth in the Temple of God) parallels the "abomination of desolation" (Matt. 24:15; cf. Dan. 9:27; 11:31; 12:11). When the Antichrist desecrates the rebuilt temple in Jerusalem, he will usurp (a position, office, power, etc.) worship for himself.

4. The Prophecy – A military might arises from the "uttermost parts of the north" of Israel as an end-time military superpower -

Scripture:

> [2]*Son of man, set thy face against Gog, the land of Magog, the chief prince of Meshech and Tubal, and prophesy against him,*
> [3]*And say, Thus saith the Lord GOD; Behold, I am against thee, O Gog, the chief prince of Meshech and Tubal:*
> Ezekiel 38:2, 3 KJV

It is imperative that there is correct interpretation and understanding of these two scriptures…

Here is how *Strong's Hebrew-Greek Dictionary* defines Gog and Magog:

1136 Gog (gogue); of Hebrew origin [1463]; Gog, a symb. Name for some future Antichrist: KJV— Gog.

3098 Magog (mag-ogue'); of Hebrew origin [4031]; Magog, a foreign nation, i.e. (figuratively) an Antichristian party: KJV— Magog.

The profit Ezekiel sees into the future, a prophetic insight into what is to happen as a future event.

- In verse-2, Ezekiel prophesied, "*set thy face against Gog*" the (symbolic name for a future Antichrist or Satan), and "the land of Magog" a (is a name reserved for any foreign nation or group of people. This foreign nation is located in the "*uttermost parts of the north*" of Israel), "the chief prince" are the (head or leaders) of "*Meshech and Tubal*" of these nations

Scripture:

> [15]*And thou shalt come from thy place out of the north parts, thou, and many people with thee, all of them riding upon horses, a great company, and a mighty army:* Ezekiel 38:15 KJV

Present Day Nations Located in the Uttermost Parts North of Israel:

Meshech and Tubal - Are always associated together in scripture
Persia - Iran (The name changed to Iran in 1935)
Cush - Sudan
Ethiopia - (part of Cush)
Put - Modern day Libya
Gomer - (Gimmerai) East Turkey near Armenia
Togarmah
Ammon, Moab and Edom - Jordan
Sheba and Dedan - Arabia near the Red Sea
Lydia and Phrygia - North East Turkey
Russia

- In verse-3, God will rise up against Satan, his leaders and his army, and He (God) will send the Son of man to defeat Satan's army against the nations that will attack Israel. Ezekiel 38:3 KJV

5. The Prophecy – The mark of the beast that will control the economy in order to operate in the earth –

Scripture:

16 And he causeth all, both small and great, rich and poor, free and bond, to receive a mark in their right hand, or in their foreheads:
17 And that no man might buy or sell, save he that had the mark, or the name of the beast, or the number of his name.
18 Here is wisdom. Let him that hath understanding count the number of the beast: for it is the number of a man; and his number is Six hundred threescore and six. Revelation 13:16-18 KJV

Will You Be Marked? :

As we see prophetic events unfold things are in the process of being setup for him, the (Antichrist) to come on the scene at his appointed time. Will you be marked? The word "*mark*" (Gr. Charagma), used to describe an *image, stamp, brand or some other mark*. The big question is when will the mark of the beast take place? The mark of the beast will begin and enforced halfway through the (Antichrist's) seven-year rule during the Great Tribulation. Can you see in (Revelation 13:17) that by controlling global trade, that the world will not be able to conduct normal everyday personal business or corporate business as it is today?

One must submit to the political and religious system of the beast. If you worship the beast and receive the mark of the beast, you will receive the complete wrath of God. The book of Revelation in the Bible gives us this strong warning. (*If any man worship the beast and his image, and receive his mark in his forehead, or in his hand,...*) he or she, too, will (*The same shall drink of the wine of the wrath of God...*) fury, which will pour out full strength into the cup of His wrath. Revelation 14:9, 10 - If you get the mark of the beast, God's complete wrath will pour out on all those that partake or accept his mark.

They Are Tracking You - Truth Revealed:

On May-10-2002, three members of a family in Florida became the first group of people to receive a biochip implanted under the skin of their body. The name of this device is a VeriChip™; it is a small radio transmitter about the size of a piece of rice injected under a person's skin. How does this device work? It transmits a unique personal ID number whenever it is within a few feet of a special receiver unit. The VeriChip's maker describes this as a radio frequency identification device (RFID) used in a variety of security scenarios, emergency and healthcare applications. The maker of this biochip is stating that this as an important medical benefit, do not believe this because this is a deception to allow this device implanted under a person's skin for identification and tracking purposes. It is imperative that we as born again believers of Jesus Christ wake up to this! Now, this is not the mark of the beast. However, could this be part of the mark of the beast, maybe or maybe not? At some point and time in the very near future, it could be part of the physical mark placed on a person's forehead or right hand. As we see events unfold things are in the process of being setup for him, the (Antichrist) to come on the scene at his appointed time. As I end with a few biblical prophecies that shall "come to pass" as prophesied in the Old Testament by the prophets, and in the New Testament it is apparent that what we are witnessing today is "end-time prophecy", come to pass is more profound than ever before. Can you see it? Can you see the signs? Will you pay attention to it!

Truth Revealed - continued:

Did your state rebel against the (Real ID Act) that the federal government is attempting to put in place? Be thankful it did, but it is not dead. Yes, many states have decided to reject the unfunded mandates of the (Real ID Act), a massive national identification program the federal government is trying to force upon the American people by attempting to implement it through the drivers licensing systems. The promotion of this program comes across as the solution to national security, identity theft, illegal immigration etc. Can you say smoke and mirrors or a trick of the enemy! The reality is that the federal government wants to force states into building a multi-billion dollar system for identifying, tracking, and controlling law-abiding citizens. Rest assured, that The Department of Homeland Security and the National Governors Association are working together to propose a revised (Real ID Act). Do not remain ignorant (not knowing) to the prophetic signs that are taking place before your very eyes. Can you see it? Now back to this prophetic night vision of future events to unfold through the spiritual insight of the (Seer), a prophet.

Would you like to know more?

[CHAPTER 5]
The Building

AGAIN, IT IS TIME for me to travel to another location. Therefore, as my heavenly transport ship fuels up, I am now instantly standing in front of what appears to be a warehouse or some sort of building. I must continue to reiterate this, that I am an observer, and a participant in this prophetic night vision. It is dark outside but there was illumination of light, and there were many people standing around. These people were not just standing around and I could hear various voices but could not make out what was stated; it was just many voices. As I continue to observe, I said to myself these people are standing in line for something. Again, I said to myself could it be food, clothing, or was it something else? I know one thing, it is apparent that these people, like me undoubtedly left behind because we were not in right standing with God, and we missed the first class flight to a better place. Here is the million-dollar question. Why were there people gathered outside of this mysterious warehouse or building, and standing in line? Were they forced or did they volunteer? All of the sudden my focus moved to something very interesting, there were numerous armed soldiers in the area, and they were heavily armed. I said to myself again, numerous armed soldiers guarding a warehouse and numerous people standing around in line. Something is not right. The one thing I notice about myself is that I am not standing in the same line as the other people, and the soldiers have not noticed that I am set apart from the others. I know I am observing; but for now, it appears as if protection is upon me or is it that they have not noticed me. I have never seen soldiers like the ones I am observing in all my life. Apparently, the soldiers are servants of the enemy, Satan! I realized in this dream that I am witnessing part of the Tribulation in action; I believe that the people are in danger because it appears as if the soldiers are holding them against there will by gunpoint.

As I stand in the midst of the night surrounded by danger from Satan's cohorts, I am wondering what is next because so many things are taking place all around me. It so astounding that I am able to operate with my senses functioning in this night vision, especially my vision, hearing and my mental thoughts. I also have the ability to hear and speak to various people in real-time, but still I am not able to see a recognizable face.

Would you like to know more?

The Chamber Transformation

As I whispered just enough to hear myself say, what is the operation of this place that resembles a warehouse? Then it began to dawn on me that this is a place, where a person's life will change eternally for the bad or good. A question was asked earlier, and the question is (*Why were there people gathered outside of this mysterious warehouse, and standing in line*)? I believe that this structure is a place to receive the mark of the beast and or a beheading chamber for those who will not accept his mark or renounce Jesus Christ. The reason why I believe that this is a place that appears as if something like this type of horrific thing to happen is because I can see through a window very clearly people, even though I was at a distance. All of the sudden the view of this window becomes closer and closer as if I am being moved closer to see more; but I did not walk closer to the building, I was moved like a chess piece into a strategic position. As I look through the window there is enough light to see on the inside of a room an apparatus hanging or suspend in the air. I attempted to make out what I was looking at, it is not very clear. All of the sudden the view of the apparatus becomes clearer. I can now see a person in a sitting position as this apparatus lowers down onto the top of the head of a person sitting in a raised chair, and when removed from the persons head, he looked towards the window and there was a mark stamped on the forehead of that person.

What I suspected was true, this building is to receive the mark of the beast and a chamber for beheading people. I heard people scream, and then all of the sudden the screams stop abruptly. I believe this is when someone lost his or her head. A visual of the beheading did not present itself, but an audio and (the type of scream) that came forth, and an abrupt ending of the scream. I believe there were quite a few people that accepted the mark of the beast, but I also believe there were many that did not accept the mark of the beast.

It says in Revelation 20:4 AMP –

> 4 *Then I saw thrones, and sitting on them were those to whom authority to act as judges and to pass sentence was entrusted. Also I saw the souls of those who had been slain with axes [beheaded] for their witnessing to Jesus and [for preaching and testifying] for the Word of God, and who had refused to pay homage to the beast or his statue and had not accepted his mark or permitted it to be stamped on their foreheads or on their hands. And they lived again and ruled with Christ (the Messiah) a thousand years.*

Note: Read the KJV of this scripture as well.

The scripture above is very important that understanding and revelation is a key factor. The people at this building are only a few that will not take the mark of the beast, and there are many others. These are some of the “Tribulation Martyrs”, who refuse to worship the beast.

What questions does this scripture raise? :

1. Who are the beheaded? It clearly states that born again believers of Jesus Christ who are still alive on the earth during the reigning of the Antichrist.
2. When are born again believers of Jesus Christ beheaded? The Antichrist's reign of terror begins at the midpoint of Daniel's Seventieth Week and runs to the beginning of the Day of the Lord, which is during the “Tribulation Period”.
3. Why are born again believers of Jesus Christ beheaded? Born again believers of Jesus Christ will be challenged for their faith in Jesus Christ, the truth of Word of God and their unwillingness to worship the Antichrist.

I want to bring this to everyone’s attention regarding this scripture. Unfortunately, this scripture does not answer a very important question. Why were born again believers of Jesus Christ resurrected at the beginning of the millennium? Perhaps some insight of this is in the Book of Revelation 6:9-11 concerning this question.

9When the Lamb broke open the fifth seal, I saw at the foot of the altar the souls of those whose lives had been

sacrificed for [adhering to] the Word of God and for the testimony they had borne.
[10]They cried in a loud voice, O [Sovereign] Lord, holy and true, how long now before You will sit in judgment and avenge our blood upon those who dwell on the earth?

[11]Then they were each given a [b]long and flowing and festive white robe and told to rest and wait patiently a little while longer, until the number should be complete of their fellow servants and their brethren who were to be killed as they themselves had been.

Revelation 6:9-11 AMP. Note: Read the KJV as well.

The similarity between the two groups of martyrs described in these two passages, allows the reader to conclude that this is the same group described in both places. This is also the "*fifth seal*" which presents the "Martyrdom of Tribulation" saints throughout the world. They will come to faith in Jesus Christ following the "rapture" or the "catching away" and many killed by satanic opposition because of their testimony of Jesus Christ. They plead for God's judgment on their unbelieving oppressors (Antichrist and his followers). In verse-11, the "white robes" depict their righteous standing before God. More saints will experience the martyrdom effect, since there is much more of the Tribulation to come. Unfortunately, the martyrs in the Book of Revelation appear to be special in that they refuse to submit to Antichrist's demand for worship and killed for it. The period beginning at the midpoint of Daniel's Seventieth Week and running until the beginning of the Day of the Lord's wrath will be the single most challenging time in human history to be a follower of Jesus Christ. During this time of faithfulness to God, and during this time of gloominess and glory up to and including the giving of their lives, God will honor them. For anyone to die as a "beheaded martyr" and resurrected again just as Jesus Christ did; near the beginning of the millennial kingdom for all to witness is certainly a great honor. Yes, their deaths are particularly violent and ruthless, which may in fact explain why the resurrection took place at the beginning of the millennial reign of Christ. In the Book of Revelation 6:11, indicates that God instructed the martyrs *(that they should rest yet for a little season* – or to wait a little while longer) so the avenging of their deaths are on those who dwell on the earth during this time. God's vengeance "shall come to pass" against Satan, his followers, who dwell on this earth, which will coincide with the battle of Armageddon that occurs at the end of the 30-day reclamation period that follows the Seventieth Week of Daniel.

Would you like to know more?

The People Recognizing Factor

As I continue to observe what is taking place in front of me at this wicked warehouse, I began noticing what women and men are wearing, recognizable clothing. I spoke out to a man that was standing in line in order to get his attention by saying hey, do I know you, but he did not respond, and when I began to pronounce his name who I thought I recognized, I could not do it. Again, access denied when it comes to this simple act. As I watched him walk through the door, he briefly turns toward me with a light grey face, which I could not recognize…

It says in Isaiah 59:1, 2 KJV –

> *1Behold, the LORD's hand is not shortened, that it cannot save; neither his ear heavy, that it cannot hear: 2But your iniquities have separated between you and your God, and your sins have hid his face from you, that he will not hear.*

…Why did he turn towards me? What could this mean? I believe that verse-2 in the above scripture answers the two questions posed. Did he willingly enter into that building not knowing what was going to happen or was he forced. This appears to be the fate of all those that are lined up at this warehouse. I also recognized the type of clothing he was wearing. This man was well dressed and had on a suit; it was light blue color with a white shirt and tie. What is interesting about describing the clothing is that there was enough light around the warehouse for me to see it and describe it. This man reminded me of a Pastor or Minister. I know this will most likely step on some toes, but there will be men and women called and chosen as Pastors by God whose walk and talk did not line up with the Word of God, and not caught up in the clouds. So many things revealed in such an unusual manner. As I continue to observe what is taking place around me, I began to become concerned about obtaining the attention of the man I called out; because of this, I brought attention to myself from the surrounding people and the guards standing outside the warehouse. All of the sudden one of the guards notices me and begins to make his way towards the area of where I was standing. When I notice what was taking place I decided to blend in more with other people because there were so many standing around waiting for there eternal fate to be decided, including me. All of the sudden; he stops and turns back towards the direction in whence he came; because the crowd began to become somewhat unruly. If it was not for the ruckus that was taking place, it could have been trouble for me. I know that it is not over regarding the guard noticing me. I believe that this distraction was on purpose.

My attention now turns back towards the entrance of the building where I see people continuing to walk inside; and as I watch this take place, I continue to say do I know him; but never able to call out the person's name or look into his face. Again, this has been the norm throughout this night vision. Well, again my attention now turns back towards the window. I say to myself, can anyone else see what is going on through this window. Could it be that I am the only one allowed to view what is happening on the inside of this building from the outside of this building? How and why is this happening? As I continue to keep my eye on the guards in the area and the number of people that were willing to take the mark of the beast or beheaded because they would not reject (Jesus Christ) disturbed me! However, I believe that my fate would not be as the others standing around this warehouse. As I suspected, the distraction did not last long the guards were still wondering whom the main person or persons in the crowd was (left behinds) calling out possible names of various people heading into the warehouse.

The Seal of God

As this night vision continues, the thought of various people receiving the mark of the beast is a very bad decision and or choice to make. However, many people will choose willingly to accept it, and there will be an attempt to force those left behind to take it. However, there will be many, that will not take or receive the mark of the beast. Well, hold up for one minute, before I go any further with this night vision, I want to elaborate on a couple of things regarding a seal and a mark stamped on someone. Moreover, there are a few seals to examine, they are extremely important and they have their place. The first question is what is the Seal of God?

God's Seal:

The seal of God is His name *...written in their foreheads.* (Revelation 14:1), and the seal of God *...is sealed the servants of our God in their foreheads.* (Revelation 7:3) - How do we get this seal or the name of God sealed on us? "Only those who love God will get His name!" Let me repeat the previous statement again, "Only those who love God will get His name!" Here it is, (*If ye love me, keep my commandments.* - John 14:15 KJV) In other words, one must keep His commandments in his heart and mind. Not only is a seal in our foreheads, but in our hand as well. Here's proof, in the Book of Isaiah 44:5 AMP – *"One will say, I am the Lord's; and another will call himself by the name of Jacob; and another will write [even brand or tattoo] upon his hand, I am the Lord's, and surname himself by the [honorable] name of Israel."* Again, here is proof that the seal of God is the hand of His people.

In this case, "*The Seal of God*" is a stamp, a seal promised by God and I believe this will still apply to many that accept Jesus Christ as there Lord and Savior left behind after the "catching away or rapture". As one continues to read further, you will discover God's seal and the mark of the beast in similar places; but their eternal destinations have different addresses assigned to them.

Note: What I would like to do is provide an example of the seal in the Kingdom of God:

The Kingdom of God Seal Illustration:

To authenticate the Seal in the Kingdom of God will boil down to the Sabbath commandment, which contains all the elements used in the Seal…

The seal states whom, what, when, where, why and how authority is given:

1. A Name = It is the Lord thy God who is sealing it
2. A Number = The seventh day
3. An Authority = A person's office or authority
4. An Authorizer = who gives this authority? God gives authority, and He is His own authority
5. Dominion and Territory = It states the realm or jurisdiction where He has authority. This is heaven, the earth, the sea, and all that is in them. Note: Yes, the Lord thy God has given man dominion over the things of the earth

6. A Duration = One day. This is the time frame of how long the authorization will last

When we understand the covenant the (legal agreement), it is the seal, God's stamp of approval stamped on us that will ensure eternal life with Him. The Lord thy God used Jesus Christ and the Holy Spirit to fulfill this covenant.

Note: At the end of this book read about the Seal of God in-depth revelation: Read Chapter 12

Note: What I would like to do now is provide an example of a seal in the world.

Worldly Seal Illustration:

To authenticate a document there are six essential elements for the seal to be authentic, for example, the Seal of the United States…

1. A Name = John F. Kennedy

2. A Number = All People

3. A Title = President of the United States

4. An Authorizer = The people

5. A Territory = The United States

6. A Duration = Time spent in office

As we see in the world the (who, what, when, where, why, and how) of authority is given to bring forth authentication to a seal of a document or an office, etc. It has the same number of (titles) but the meaning is different when it comes to the Kingdom of God. Now, it is time to continue reading…

The Mark of the Beast

Now the mark of the beast has its place as well and as one has read earlier, (*And that no man might buy or sell, save he that had the mark, or the name of the beast, or the number of his name.*) Revelation 13: 17 KJV as one reads on, take notice of the same six elements that applies to the mark of the beast. Do you want proof that this lines up with the written Word of God?

Note: What I would like to do now is provide an example of the mark of the beast:

Mark of the Beast Illustration:

As you read on, scriptures provide proof to back up this illustration.

1. A Name = *...and upon his heads the name of blasphemy.* (Revelation 13: 1 KJV)

2. A Number = *Here is wisdom. Let him that hath understanding count the number of the beast: for it is the number of a man; and his number is Six hundred threescore and six.* (Revelation 13: 18 KJV)

3. A Title and Authority = *And they worshipped the dragon which gave power unto the beast:* (Revelation 13: 4 KJV)

4. An Authorizer = *...the Dragon gave authority to the beast:* ... (Revelation 13: 4 KJV)

5. Dominion and Territory = *...and power was given him over all kindred's, and tongues, and nations.* (Revelation 13: 7 KJV)

6. Duration = *...and power was given unto him to continue forty and two months.* (Revelation 13: 5 KJV)

Can one see how Satan has copied and mocked God with a seal and or mark in the forehead and on the right hand? What a counterfeiter, a knock-off Satan is, he hates God so much that his desire is to be like God in every way, that a permanent mark resides in his devilish spirit and soul forever. However, Satan can never be God or defeat God. Even in this night vision, I truly believe that my eternal fate is different, it has to be from the other people entering that building and that I will not be taking the mark of the beast, but I believe in the end I will receive the "*promised seal*" with an "*inheritance*" and an everlasting seal of God. It says in Ephesians 1: 11-13 AMP

> 11 *In Him we also were made [God's] heritage (portion) and we obtained an inheritance; for we had been foreordained (chosen and appointed beforehand) in accordance with His purpose, Who works out everything in agreement with the counsel and design of His [own] will,*
>
> 12 *So that we who first hoped in Christ [who first put our confidence in Him have been destined and appointed to] live for the praise of His glory!*
>
> 13 *In Him you also who have heard the Word of Truth, the glad tidings (Gospel) of your salvation, and have believed*

in and adhered to and relied on Him, were stamped with the seal of the long-promised Holy Spirit.

It is now time for this night vision to continue... As I continue to observe the believable scenes through the window of this building, it dawned on me that I must get away from this place as soon as possible before one or more of the guards notice me again. Moments after speaking this, the guards again have turned their attention towards me. Two guards begin to walk towards the area that I am standing in. They were dressed in black clothing and were heavily armed, but I was not able to see their faces. One of the guards alerted another guard and now three of them are heading in my direction. Yes, they have spotted me and one of them shouts aloud, there he is over there, get him! The guard points in my direction and they began pushing people out of the way because they were determined to capture me. As this is taking place, I am wondering why it is difficult for me to move with quickness. Earlier times in this night vision I notice that God transported me to another location, will this be the case in this instance? The thoughts that are running through my mind are unreal especially in this dream realm. I notice that God is not transporting me this time, which is very surprising, so I began to force my way through the crowd of people in order to escape from whatever those guards have in stored for me. The crowd of the people are just looking in confusion, scared, but not attempting to stop the guards or me. For some odd reason I am moving very slowly, it is tough running in this dream realm. It is as if my capture will surely be inevitable by Satan's army. This surely cannot be! As I look back at there grayish faces, I see no eyes, or a mouth, but they can speak; no expression just a dark grayish face determined to catch me. I noticed that they are gaining ground on me. As I turn my head forward, I continue to run but what I see in front of me is pure darkness, no illumination of light. What is the meaning of this, no escape! As I am running, I can still hear the voices of the guards saying get him! Get him! Apparently, they knew that something was special about me compared to the other people. Did the guards know that I was an observer sent there by God to report to the people in the earthly realm of what shall "come to pass" in the very near future? I believe the answer to this question is yes, they knew. As I continue to run towards the nothingness, the darkness, all of the sudden I stopped running in my tracks. Their must be a reason why I stopped running. Was it fear of the unknown, the darkness in front of me or was something else in stored for me? Well, I turned towards the direction of the lead guard out of the three and began running towards him. Even in this night vision, I really had no idea what is about to happen. The guard that I was running towards was tall in stature and as stated earlier, he is heavily armed. As the distance closed for the two of us to engage each other in what I believe was to fight or be captured, but in an instant God transported me to another location. The enemy did not capture me, behead me nor was the mark of the beast stamped on me or planted in me.

Would you like to know more?

[CHAPTER 6]

It Is 5:10 AM

I ACTUALLY NOTICED a delay in my transport location while in this night vision, a delay in time. I did not wake up immediately per say. I could still see that area of that scene for a couple of seconds like a portal closing up. However, God did transport me to a familiar place, and I awakened in my bedroom but trembling with the fear of God in me. I am able to remember everything; it is still fresh in my mind, everything that happened in real-time. Although my eyes were now open, and awake I could actually replay the scenes just like a movie displayed on a screen. I was shaking all over and I did not desire to go back to sleep because of what I experienced in this night vision just revealed to me. This night vision stayed with me throughout the day, that night, and for the next few days. In an instant, I could still replay it. I know that this night vision is permanent, archived in the video vault of my heart and mind. To my surprise, I awoke in the same position that I fell off to sleep in from the previous night. As I turned over on my left side to look at the clock sitting on the nightstand, I could clearly see the red glowing (LED's), the time read exactly 5:10am in the morning. It did not feel as if I had been sleeping for six hours and ten minutes. It felt more as if I had been sleeping for one hour. Time does not matter in the dream realm, because it does not exist there. It is apparent that "*God did not come out of time, but time came out of Him*", especially when He is showing one something prophetic and of significant importance because everything is on His divine timing. It says in... Ecclesiastes 3:1 KJV - [1]*To every thing there is a season, and a time to every purpose under the heaven*:

It was still dark in the room but enough light for me to see what I needed to do. Therefore, I reached over and turned on the lamp that was sitting on the nightstand and began to sit up in bed in order to gather myself so that I can figure out what to say and what to do next...

She Is Still Here

After sitting up for a few minutes, I decided to turn and reach over to make sure that my wife Beckie is still lying in the bed next to me. To my relief, as the title reads, (she is still here)! I almost came to tears at that very moment. With quickness, I reached over and nudged her, but she did not wake up on the first nudge. I nudged her again for the second time, and she said what is it? My reply to her was, Beckie, you are not going to believe the dream I just had! She said what dream! My response to her was the dream about the rapture. I was not "caught up" in the clouds, but you (Beckie) were! She was surprised and speechless by the statement I made. I said to her forgive me of any offenses that I have made against you, and I said to her, I must repent as well. I also need to ask God for forgiveness first! She said huh! I was not "caught up" because of a disagreement we had and I escalated it to another level, and that day out of nowhere it happened, the rapture, the catching away! Her response was Oh WOW! At that time, I said to her that I am afraid; I do not desire to be on the left behind list. As we were both silent for a moment, we looked at each other bewildered because of what took place during the night, and what I shared with her regarding this night vision. All of the sudden, my wife says, God just revealed to you a prophetic dream of what will take place in the future, and you must write it down in your journal right now! My response to her statement was, why would God reveal such a night vision or dream to me, and her response was that He only reveals things like that to the chosen ones, especially (to the prophet first) those He can trust with something as important as this dream. I really believe God knows that I will share the truth to all the world that will believe and receive what He (God) revealed to me. Immediately, I pulled out my journal and began to write down what God revealed to me in the night vision. While writing the detailed information down, I could not stop thinking about why I missed that first flight nor was I a partaker of the "catching away" with my wife or the others that instantly vanished in a blink-of-an-eye.

Then it dawned on me that the night vision revealed to me by God is for me to share with the world of what is to come in the future, that the "rapture" or "catching away" is real. In addition to this, it was to let me know that I must continue to line my talk and walk up with the truth of the written Word of God on a daily basis. For those who do not think or believe that it takes all of that, you are mistaken because it does. It truly must be a life style in order to not only get a first class ticket for the flight, but also maintain right standing with God in order to keep your first class ticket for the flight. Yes, God revealed the night vision to me. Yes, I was an observer and a participant. Yes, God can trust me with true detailed occurrences, but I could still be on the left behind list if I do not continue to stay in the Word of God and live it! It says in verse…

> [12]*It has trained us to reject and renounce all ungodliness (irreligion) and worldly (passionate) desires, to live discreet (temperate, self-controlled), upright, devout (spiritually whole) lives in this present world,*

> [13]*Awaiting and looking for the [fulfillment, the realization of our] blessed hope, even the glorious appearing of our*

great God and Savior Christ Jesus (the Messiah, the Anointed One),

[14]*Who gave Himself on our behalf that He might redeem us (purchase our freedom) from all iniquity and purify for Himself a people [to be peculiarly His own, people who are] eager and enthusiastic about [living a life that is good and filled with] beneficial deeds.* Titus 2:12-14 AMP – Read the KJV as well

When one reads the above scriptures, something should jump off the page with understanding and revelation! Verse-12 sums it up very clearly, it instructs us of how we should be living our lives by staying… *"Spiritually whole"; lives in this present world.* As I continued to write down what God revealed to me in this night vision; I am surprised at the details of what He (God) allowed me to see compared to what He (God) did not allow me to see. It is amazing how the Lord thy God operates in the spiritual realm, the vision and dream realm, and this physical realm. I wrote this earlier that no one is going to believe what I am sharing, the words written in this book. I pray that as a prophet and mouth piece for God that I speak the truth of the Word of God and convey it to all those that will believe it, receive it, and apply written in front of those that read this book. However, there is one question in Christendom, that is often stated, and the question is, are you rapture ready? I truly believe that most born again believers of Jesus Christ will answer yes to this question. On the other hand, just because one is a born again believer of Jesus Christ does not equate to a guarantee of being "caught up". Most of you will cringe at the sentence you just read. A Christian can backslide (step back into sin), not repent, not ask for forgiveness and not have the love of God in them. It really does require a lot more than just going to Church and treating people nice. Yes, there are other religions on this earth, but there is only one-way to the Father (John 14:6) in heaven. I must not leave out those that do not believe in God, because there are many. So, what then is their belief actually comprised or consist of? I believe all of it is their unbelief that a creator (God) exists; or the Bible (scriptures) contradicts itself, morality, and many other reasons. Of course, there is more that I could expound on, but that is another book. As I end the chapter of this book, it is interesting that at this current time, I can still click the play button and the video of this night vision will began to play all over again.

Would you like to know more?

[CHAPTER 7]
Are You Scared Yet

I KNOW THAT BEING SCARED or fearful is not of God, but if this does not raise any concerns about what is contained or written here it should, if you are a born again believer of Jesus Christ and you believe what the covenant Word of God says regarding the "rapture" or "catching away". Here is the warning, it says in... Proverbs 1:7 KJV - [7]*The fear of the LORD is the beginning of knowledge: but fools despise wisdom and instruction.* What is (*the fear of the LORD*) that this scripture is talking about? I believe it is the submission to the Lord thy God, His ways and His revelation. Huh... here it is, when someone has fear of something or is afraid of something, I believe two things occur. Either the person is going to *run from it* or *submit to it*. Pay attention to the latter part of the italicized (*submit to it*) this is a healthy fear to act in an appropriate manner towards it, which is (*the fear of the Lord*). What is (*the beginning of knowledge*) that this scripture is talking about? Pay attention to (*the beginning*) because it is reverential awe and controlling principle of wisdom.

However, for the unbeliever, the fear of God is the fear of the judgment of God and eternal death, which is eternal separation from God. Read Luke 12:5, Hebrews 10:31 KJV - Are you scared yet? Why is this one of the chapters in this book? It is here for the reader to obtain knowledge, wisdom, and instruction of the truth of the written Word of God. Yes, their will be many who will disagree with everything written here, but one must stand and not waiver from what the covenant Word of God says. I also know their are many that believe all that the Word of God says, and will gravitate to not only the black ink on the pages written here, but the insight of the content there of, and how it aligns itself with prophecy from the (Basic Instructions Before Leaving Earth - Bible) manual. Therefore, I say this, get "*Caught Up Night Vision Revealed*" and do not miss your first class flight because no one knows the day or the hour!

Now, here are three powerful scriptures regarding (*the fear of the Lord*) that I believe play a role in this night vision:

Reference Scriptures -

1. [10] *The fear of the LORD is the beginning of wisdom: and the knowledge of the holy is understanding.* Proverbs 9:10 KJV – Read the AMP version as well

2. [27] *The fear of the LORD is a fountain of life, to depart from the snares of death.* Proverbs 14:27 KJV – Read the AMP version as well

3. [23] *The fear of the LORD tendeth to life: and he that hath it shall abide satisfied; he shall not be visited with evil.* Proverbs 19:23 KJV – Read the AMP version as well

There are many other scriptures that can be used pertaining to (*the fear of the Lord*), but the ones listed above have come forth. As one meditates and ponders on these three scriptures by speaking them, rooting them deeply into one's (spirit-man, soul, and heart-mind) by applying them on a daily basis, so that manifestation of them comes forth. Are you scared yet? I know this chapter title is (Are You Scared Yet), but this must come forth because of the time and season we are truly living in. Here are the signs, because the Apostle Paul said *...that in the last days perilous times shall come*. Here it is...

- Many people have lost their retirement to corporate greed and corruption. (Prophecy fulfilled in this generation). Can you see it?

- Corrupt leaders, are revealed more so now than ever before. (Prophecy fulfilled now in this generation). Can you see it?

- Neon signs, billboards, television, and the Internet etc., proclaiming our sinful, godless nature. (Prophecy fulfilled now in this generation). Can you see it?

- Financial melt down. (Prophecy fulfilled now in this generation). Can you see it?

- New age movement that brings in an increasing number of mystics, a higher power without God, Transcendental Meditation that claims to be the enlightened ones. (Prophecy fulfilled more so now than ever before in this generation). Can you see it?

Here it is; they are some of the most influential and educated people in our societies, and yet most lack truth and that truth is the covenant Word of God. Their will be many that will read this book and this statement and fully disagree with it, and that is truly OK. Here it is again, it says…

Reference Scriptures –

> [1] *But understand this, that in the last days will come (set in) perilous times of great stress and trouble [hard to deal with and hard to bear].* (Prophecy fulfilled right now)
>
> [2] *For people will be lovers of self and [utterly] self-centered, lovers of money and aroused by an inordinate [greedy] desire for wealth, proud and arrogant and contemptuous boasters. They will be abusive (blasphemous, scoffing), disobedient to parents, ungrateful, unholy and profane.* (Prophecy fulfilled right now)
>
> [3] *[They will be] without natural [human] affection (callous and inhuman), relentless (admitting of no truce or appeasement); [they will be] slanderers (false accusers, troublemakers), intemperate and loose in morals and conduct, uncontrolled and fierce, haters of good.* (Prophecy fulfilled right now)
>
> [4]*[They will be] treacherous [betrayers], rash, [and] inflated with self-conceit. [They will be] lovers of sensual pleasures and vain amusements more than and rather than lovers of God.* (Prophecy fulfilled right now)

> [5] *For [although] they hold a form of piety (true religion), they deny and reject and are strangers to the power of it [their conduct belies the genuineness of their profession]. Avoid [all] such people [turn away from them].* (Prophecy fulfilled right now)
>
> [6] *For among them are those who worm their way into homes and captivate silly and weak-natured and spiritually dwarfed women, loaded down with [the burden of their] sins [and easily] swayed and led away by various evil desires and seductive impulses.* (Prophecy fulfilled right now)
>
> [7] *[These weak women will listen to anybody who will teach them]; they are forever inquiring and getting information, but are never able to arrive at a recognition and knowledge of the Truth.* (Prophecy fulfilled right now)

II Timothy 3:1-7 AMP – Read the KJV version as well

As you look at the first four versus 1-4 it expounds on the following…

1. The Last Days – began with the birth of our Lord Jesus Christ, and this will culminate into the glorious return to the earth to setup His kingdom.

2. The Prophecy of Perilous Times – indicates that apostasy which we see and is more prevalent now than ever before will characterize the final days of the Church age.

Now, as you look at the next three versus 5-7 it expounds on the following…

3. A form of godliness – is merely religion without power or spiritual life. There is no real or true relationship with God. Turn away from false teachers.

4. Ever learning and never able to come to the knowledge of the truth – there is no-intense study, but some esoteric quest for truth apart from God's Word.

As one can see it is no longer of the prophecy is going to happen because the fulfilling of prophecy is taking place right now because it always is fulfilling itself. It appears as if it has accelerated because the scriptures you just read are truly taking place simultaneously. Now, allow me to say this, it is not just II Timothy 3:1-7, but another chapter and scriptures where prophecies fulfilled are unfolding right now…

Prophecies Fulfilled Now & To Come

I shall begin in (our present age – New Testament) because the (Old Testament) prophesied the coming of the Son of man and the End-Of-The-Church-Age.

New Testament:

I. Matthew 24:1-4

1) When shall these things be?

2) What shall be the signs of thy coming?

- The growing economic strength and military might of China
- The U.S. National debt load
- Europe's financial crisis
- Natural disasters – Earthquakes in diver's places like (Haiti). Weather changes, that include the increase and intensity of tornadoes, thunderstorms etc. A shift in the weather pattern is already prevalent as seasons run into seasons
- The political change in Europe
- A change to a global currency is work in progress (One World Currency)

- Iran's nuclear capability and facilities which may come under attack sometime in the near future by the US and or Israel

- Continued and increased terrorism

3) When is the end of "*The Church Age*"?

II. Matthew 24:5-14

1) Many shall come in my name

2) Rumors of wars

3) Famines and pestilences

4) Beginning of sorrows (birth pangs)

5) Martyrdom and the rise of false prophets and the abound of iniquity

6) The gospel preached in all the world

As mentioned, earlier in this book the gospel preached in the entire world is a fulfilled prophecy that is taking place right now according to Acts 20:24 by grace. There are many prophecies not yet fulfilled, but rest assured, they will, it is just a matter of when. As one reads, other prophecies fulfilled right now are prevalent and others shall "come to pass"…

III. Matthew 24:33-42

1) Signs of Christ's return (the revelation of Christ), and not the "catching away or rapture"

   - Israel's return to the Promised Land
   - The obvious acceleration of lawlessness
   - Aggression against Israel
   - Cashless trading
   - Increased apostasy and disobedience
   - The socio-religious climate (preparation of the one world order and the one world religion or Church)
   - Rapid acceleration of life threatening conditions (nuclear annihilation, pollution, diseases, turbulent weather, and a population explosion etc.) just to name a few

2) This generation shall not pass until all these things are fulfilled

3) No man knows the day. The Father only knows the time of Christ's return

4) Comparison to the days of Noah and Lot (Ref. Luke 17:26-30)

5) The last generation is pleasure-oriented and self-gratifying by eating, drinking and marrying and giving in marriage or (carrying on the normal course) of life without heeding the impending judgment

6) Knew not or unprepared for the coming of the Son of man

Nonetheless, I will stop right here as this can go into another book, but I believe that when you align what is taking place in the earth it is aligned with the scriptures that there are multiple prophecies fulfilled right now. Again, we must wake-up, the alarm has sounded, and it is taking place right in front of us. "Can you see it" and "Are You Scared Yet"?

Would you like to know more?

[CHAPTER 8]

Run To God to Survive If Left Behind

DID YOU MISS YOUR FLIGHT; or is it that you never had a ticket and left behind? Are you in need of a survival manual? What you have on your bookshelf or on the coffee table, it cannot compare to this manual. If so, I pray that you already have this manual in your possession because you may not be able to purchase it from a bookstore, your local library or online because it will not be readily available or obtainable from these places because Satan and his cohorts removed them. Have you not figured it out yet? It is happening already, how the Bible removal from various places is prevalent, ah like the courthouse. Can you see it? However, one can check the local Church (future prophetic event) if it is not too late, but make sure you have the correct version of this manual. I highly recommend the (KJV) version or the one and only original, the (Geneva Bible of 1599). Yes, you got it right, it is a survival guide called the (Basic Instructions Before Leaving Earth) manual. In addition to having this manual, it is imperative that one truly believe, turn to God, make Jesus Christ your Lord and savior of your life, and repent in a hurry during this time frame because those left behind, as we are "changed" in a moment and the "catching away" will truly be living in the "Tribulation" period! When Jesus said in … John 14:2, 3 about "*I go to prepare a place for you*", He was not kidding! Do not wait for this point and time but prepare yourself for the place that Jesus has already prepared for you. I know I said run to God, one should turn this into an all out *sprint*!

The Political Unstable Climate

As we see this prophetic time unfold before us, it is apparent that what we are seeing right now in the world is a lack of true leadership in the United States. The United States has steadily lost its influence among many nations because (God) is removed from the foundation it was built on, and most of our political leaders in the United States have no moral center (values) to direct their decision making process. What we see is distrust, dislike, and a dark vision instead of a vision of light. This is not just an American phenomenon but is a common theme in Europe, Asia, South America, and this does include the entire world, as we know it. Because of the lack of true leadership, a vacuum or a void now exist in the world, and because of this vacuum or void an opportunity will present itself for a man (who we know as the Antichrist) to arise and come forth. This man the (Antichrist) will be very charismatic, confident, intelligent, will have solutions for the bad economic conditions and attractive to people of all nations. Shortly after the "catching away" and based on the prophecies in the Bible (See Revelation 13:7-9 and Daniel 7:21 and continue reading to 22) such a man will arise and come forth, and he will be successful in uniting the various nations to rule as a dictator during the time of the "Tribulation" period. Here it is… (Unbelievers of the world will be deceived into believing that the (Antichrist) is a god –

Second Thessalonians 2:4, 11 and (*those names written in the book of life will refuse to worship the Antichrist/Beast. The Antichrist/Beast will persecute the saints of God, and exercise power throughout the world*). One will have to locate this in the scriptures and get understanding and revelation of it. Some of the things presented here happened prior to the "rapture or catching away" and during the "tribulation" but rest assured it will happen. Ask yourself these questions. What am I running to right now? What will I run to if left behind to endure the calamities described in this end-time Church age and what the Bible says about the current prophetic times we are all currently living in? Do not be a head in the clouds or a left behind with your head in the sand Christian either, see what is taking place now.

Would you like to know more?

[CHAPTER 9]

Stay Out Of the Dark

WHAT IS THE DARK OR DARKNESS that each of us should stay out of? Before we begin, diving into what we should stay out of, a definition of (dark and or darkness) in the spiritual sense is necessary. Because this is not the kind of dark or darkness that when the lights go out, or when one is about to go to bed or walk through a dark alley, and yes it has its place; but it is the type of (dark or darkness) that can separate us from the light that each of us should gravitate to. Now, let us look at true believers of Jesus Christ compared to unbelievers of Jesus Christ when it comes to the definition of the word dark or darkness. This also must be included, that there are some born again believers of Jesus Christ walking in darkness, and yes, it can happen, but with repentance and deliverance this can change. There is a difference between the mindset of true believers and unbelievers regarding Jesus Christ. The difference is like night and day. Born again believers have the light of Jesus Christ that shines within their soul; but unbelievers continued to engage in and captured by darkness. Since unbelievers are in darkness, they do not hope for, nor look for, or wait for the return of Jesus Christ. As with true believers, they are hoping for, looking for the return of Jesus Christ. At least true believers should be. If only those that missed the flight, including the observer and participant in this night vision truly understood, what it really meant to stay out of the dark.

However, in the (Strong Concordance) it says that darkness is…

> Cognate: 4653 *skotía* (a *feminine* noun) – *darkness*, a brand of moral, spiritual *obscurity* (i.e. which blocks the light of God when faith is lacking). It also says that… *skótos* ("darkness").

Well, we are all born into sin or (darkness) according to Psalm 51:5; because it is our sin nature, yes, it is in our (Adam seed) DNA. On the other hand, there is God's nature, spiritual DNA to counteract the sin nature DNA. You may be asking where's this going, it is (The blindness of their heart/mind, darkened in there understanding, their intelligence, or perceptions) which refers to the hardness of will. Many in the past, present and future have gone and will go against the divine will of God, and has separated himself or herself from God's life through ignorance or (not knowing), hardened hearts and disobedience (*…and the darkness comprehended it not*. See John 1:5) – Walking in darkness coupled with disobedience to the Word of God will be the reason, why many people will not partake in the "catching away" as prophesied. When one looks at darkness it is not our friend, it leads us down the wrong path, it is not the way and it can cost you your life eternally, but the illumination of light, the covenant Word of God can overtake darkness. Therefore, presented here are two paths to choose from, and as a *free moral agent* the decision and or choice are two, there is no in between, gray area or straddling the fence as the secular world would use. Unfortunately, these sayings have made there way into Christendom just like witchcraft (demonic forces, and spiritual darkness) in the Church.

Path-1:

But the path of the just is as the shining light ... - Proverbs 4:18

Path-2:

The way of the wicked is as darkness: ... - Proverbs 4:19

It is emphasized here as conflict and struggle between the two scriptures, embrace path-1 and avoid path-2 at all cost. As far as this night vision is concern, there was a level of spiritual darkness present, and it was un-forgiveness and no repentance or (no change of mind, or turning away from) that came forth which boiled down to disobedience revealed; even for the ones gathered in many places throughout this true experience of this night vision. Therefore, what is darkness, and what is light? These two opposing forces that constantly conflict but they both have their place as well. For example, let us call darkness (spiritual darkness) which is not passive; but active and is active on a level promoted by spiritual forces under the leadership of Satan our adversary. However, when viewed on a human level, darkness is not only the absence of knowledge (ignorance or not knowing) but has a personal and active opposition to the precepts and truth of the covenant Word of God. As one sees, where we are in this appointed time and season those that believe Satan is real, will discern how he is exercising his demonic spiritual power in the earth more now than ever before by promoting both ignorance, fear, poverty, sickness, witchcraft and human opposition with more intensity and cunningness. Well, let us further look at (dark or darkness) and (light) again by bringing additional scriptures to *light*. When one continues to examine these opposing forces, there is also a connection with "thine eye" and of course, the darkening of the mind mentioned earlier in this chapter.

Here it is. It says in…

> Matthew 6:22, 23 AMP - [22] *The eye is the lamp of the body. So if your eye is sound, your entire body will be full of light.*
>
> [23] *But if your eye is unsound, your whole body will be full of darkness. If then the very light in you [your conscience] is darkened, how dense is that darkness!*

Again, we see the connection between verse 22 and 23 because the previous verse leads one up to what Jesus is bringing forth. Jesus is giving an example of a physical eye by linking it to what happens in our heart, mind, and soul. If you are walking in the dark or darkness as written here, it is imperative that one does not allow the darkness within to be a light. This type of lifestyle can cause one to miss that first class flight mentioned earlier; remember, the "catching away". If you missed it, it is OK just go back, read it again, and again, and again until it affects the spirit-man, the heart-mind in a way that it wakes one up from sleeping.

Demonic Spirits the Take Over

As one continues to read this chapter, it is apparent that when one operates or walks in spiritual darkness lead by demonic forces an operation that one should not operate in. Yes, this is witchcraft! The title, "Demonic Spirits the Take Over", used in order to get your attention. However, demonic spirits are disembodied spirits of the (pre Adam) race that are at work virtually everywhere in the world today. However, it is not theory but true operation in the earth and in a realm lead by Satan our adversary and by those who have allowed demonic spirits to take up residence on the inside of them, instead of the true light of Jesus Christ residing on the inside. One may be asking, how this is related to *"Caught Up | Night Vision Revealed"*? Its relationship is to those that were still here after the "catching away" and while it was happening, those screaming in the streets because various people vanished, those gathered in the gymnasium attempting to hear the Word of God, those wondering around in the park, those standing around that building or warehouse, and those taking the mark of the beast. As this chapter ends and another one begins, I really do hope that as one read and meditate on this and what it pertains to "Stay out Of the Dark" that it takes root in one's heart and mind. I must say that this is no joke, either one believes it or not it shall come a time, very soon that we will see the coming of the Son of man in this generation. I ask that one return to the beginning of this book and read what God revealed to his prophet, so that I not only share it with everyone; but it is used as "*preparation*" of what is to come.

One must do all he or she can do in order to make sure that things in one's life is aligned with what the Word of God says so that whoever is reading this book and believes shall not be left behind. It truly is the right time and season for this night vision revealed to come forth for all to read.

Would you like to know more?

[CHAPTER 10]
Wake Up Do Not Remain Asleep

IN THIS NIGHT VISION, I was asleep which has its place because this was the time the Lord thy God used to get my attention to reveal what he had for me to share with the world that would believe it. After the night vision, I awoke with an astounding true prophetic message to share. However, this is not the asleep or the awaking I am referring too. It is to wake those up from the sleep, which the enemy has over many in this world. A type of sleep that has people heads in the clouds, walking in a daze, confusion, head in the sand and fatal distractions. Has the enemy put you in a deep sleep of unawareness and darkness or blinded your mind? Here it is… It was like this in the time of Noah when people spurned his warnings; but judgment did finally befall. Furthermore, it was also the same in the days of Lot, the people ate, they drank, they bought, they sold, they planted, and they built… and did nothing else. If one, would like to know about this then read the book of Luke chapter 17, starting with verse-26 and read to the end of the chapter. In this night vision, many were asleep and did not believe what the Bible prophesied, and was not "caught up" with others who did believe it. Is this where you are in this prophetic time and season? Everyday in the forefront of a true believers thought it should be this. "*Today is the day that Jesus Christ will appear in the sky to deliver all true believers up to be with Him (God) forever*". However, this is not possible if the enemy has one asleep and walking in darkness! As one looks around at what is happening on and in the earth, it is apparent that not just small amounts of Christians are asleep, but a large number are. This includes those that do not believe in God or has not confessed that Jesus is Lord and savior in their life, unbelievers. What can wake one up from this heart/mind and sight blinding effect that the enemy has over a large number of people? What will it take; a serious disease or sicknesses like cancer, a life and death situation with oneself or with a family member? What will it take to get your attention? As one reads this prophetic night vision event that took place in real time, and I am attempting to wake the people up now before time runs out. As these questions are answered, their will be many that will disagree. However, the covenant Word of God and prayer are keys to your salvation. This can start with the person that is reading this book. Now this applies to the body of Christ and in this case unbelievers of Jesus Christ as well. Take heed to this…

It says… in the Book of Ephesians 5:14 AMP - *Therefore He says, Awake, O sleeper, and arise from the dead, and Christ shall shine (make day dawn) upon you and give you light*. What is stated here is that exposing sin is beneficial, and the Lord thy God invites the unbeliever (thou that sleep) to turn from the sin, the darkness (arise from the dead), with the promise that (the sinner) will be granted the spiritual enlightenment and help needed (Christ shall give the light). My brothers and sister, I want to take you back to the people that were walking around in the park in a daze in this night vision revealed occurrence. This was the type of sleep, which the enemy wanted to keep many people from waking up. The expected end that the (Antichrist) is offering is to chain the souls of as many people he can get his hands on to join him in eternity, which is in Hell! Still many continued not to seek the covenant Word of God, still no confessing that Jesus Christ is Lord and savior, still no prayer life, still disobedient, even after these prophesied events continue to fulfill themselves right before their very eyes. Hmmm, as I begin to think about what I am writing here, it dawns on me that I too am one of the ones subjected to darkness in this night vision; but as stated earlier, I am an observer and a participant. I believe that this came forth in order for me to see what happens when one turns his or her back away from the covenant Word of God. Here is why it is so important right now to wake up! As we look at this right now, the Lord thy God knew it would take signs, a shaking in the spirit realm and the earth to wake us up, and remind us that we have a lot of work to do in this time and season.

Many Old Testament prophets saw visions, dreams and prophesied biblical prophecies about our future on earth. The Lord thy God inspired these Men of God to include it in the Bible and since God is an all-knowing spiritual being we should trust and study along with the rest of the covenant Word of God. However, it is increasingly obvious that the time of our Lord's coming is drawing near. We see prophecy fulfilled daily, and at a faster pace than ever before. Whether you believe in a pre-tribulation "rapture" or the "catching away", or believe Christians will be a witness to the full tribulation, wrath, and final judgments. The truth of the matter is that birth pains are apparent in the earth and the signs of the times will have the same effect on all of us. However, true and real Christians, Apostles, Prophets, Evangelist, Ministers or Pastors etc., of the gospel, should be motivated to save as many souls as they can in the time that we have left in this "End-Of-The-Church-Age" and prophetic time frame. As we examine what the Great Commission says, as disciples, we should be disseminating the good news to all nations, which is taking place right now and bring the true message of salvation through Jesus Christ to all people. Since the Church is "caught up" before the tribulation, it is important that we leave behind an explanation for the trials and judgments for those left behind will face because their will be many because their eternal life will be at stake. How else will they recognize the deception of the Antichrist, by seeking the truth of the Bible, the covenant Word of God? Those who are left here to endure the tribulation will need to be prepared to not only share the message of salvation, but share the reasons for God's judgment and have faith to hold it up as further proof of their need to be saved. Right now, the Lord is looking for a "Few Good Men and Women" who will carry the Gospel and prophetic word; but one must be awake in order to operate in this type of ministry or walk in this type of office. It is now time for you to wake up and not remain asleep!

Now, let us continue with your wake up process. What must one do to truly awake from the sleep that the enemy has over many people? It starts with an expression that has become common: "a wake-up call". Of course, you remember this expression; it is what hotels use when they called your room at a certain time. Just like this night vision revelation it is not the hotel calling; but the Lord does have all of our names and he is calling you right now! The Apostle Paul had "a wake-up call"; we see this on his road trip to Damascus where he had a God encounter and a true transformation event too take place in his life. Hmmm, right before his eyes... Do you get it? The Process: The Apostle Paul said... This means to renew your mind so that transformation comes forth, and renew the spirit of your mind with the covenant Word of God daily.

> 14 *Therefore He says, Awake, O sleeper, and arise from the dead, and Christ shall shine (make day dawn) upon you and give you light.*
>
> 15 *Look carefully then how you walk! Live purposefully and worthily and accurately, not as the unwise and witless, but as wise (sensible, intelligent people),*
>
> 16 *Making the very most of the time [buying up each opportunity], because the days are evil.*
>
> 17 *Therefore do not be vague and thoughtless and foolish, but understanding and firmly grasping what the will of the Lord is.*
>
> 18 *And do not get drunk with wine, for that is debauchery; but ever be filled and stimulated with the [Holy] Spirit.*
>
> Ephesians 5:14-18 AMP

Just from these five scriptures alone says this…

1. Verse 14 – Wake up, arise from being asleep
2. Verse 15 – See, walk and be wise, or "therefore watch carefully how you live"
3. Verse 16 – Redeeming the time, or "making the most of every opportunity" assigns a reason to correct sin in ones life because this is taking place during these days are so evil
4. Verse 17 – Understanding the will of the Lord
5. Verse 18 – Be sober by living under the influence of the Holy Spirit. Be filled with the life of God through Jesus Christ, character, and virtues

Hmmm, you have just received "a wake-up call". Now believe it, receive it through faith and the blood of Jesus Christ!

Would you like to know more?

[CHAPTER 11]

The Enemy Has Deceived You

IF YOU BELIEVE that you cannot be deceived, well the enemy has already deceived you! These two scriptures mentioned in the Book of Matthew 24:24 and 25 still applies in today's New Testament. As one looks at what these two types of teachers would reason that the elect could not be deceived because they are the elect (chosen by God)! Well, this is not quite true because they too can be deceived. However, in today's vernacular of this type of circular reasoning or logic has become the thought in the mind of those deceived? No, not all the elect will be lost, but many of them will be deceived, as Satan's cohorts, demonic spirits are set loose to do their evil in the earth, in this time and season we are in. As these demonic spirits seek out physical bodies to reside in and cause havoc and calamity, it is apparent that dealing with this is necessary to loose their hold on many possessed by them. This is truly an all out warfare and it starts with deception. The night vision revealed does not stop here, this prophetic message continues… As I always say, “would you like to know more”? Just like those left behind, the enemy deceived them and is deceiving many people right now, including some of the elect as mentioned earlier, but not all. There are quite a few men and women of God, that are in tuned to what is taking place on and in the earth and in the dimension of the spirit realm.

> **24** For there shall arise false Christs, and false prophets, and shall shew great signs and wonders; insomuch that, if it were possible, they shall deceive the very elect.
>
> **25** Behold, I have told you before.
>
> Matthew 24:24, 25 KJV

This is why as born again believers of Jesus Christ we must be on alert and capable of perceiving by sight (spiritually) or some other sense (spiritual discernment) what is taking place in the earth and spiritual wickedness in high places. As one has read in the last chapter, “a wake-up call” is at hand because the end of the Church age is now! Let us expound further on how the enemy is deceiving many today… If you are saying, how is this so? How does this relate to this prophetic night vision? In many ways, there is a relationship, and that is why many left behind will have to endure the tribulation. Well, I am going to share with all that is reading this book, at least five ways how the enemy is doing his job!

Five Ways How the Enemy Is Deceiving Today:

1. Same packaged lie, differently wrapped – Aged old lies disguising them in a subtle manner, gradually introducing them to even those to believe the lies instead of the infallible truth and authority of the Word of God. The enemy presents a false vision for global unity by desiring to bring the entire world's religions and philosophies together as one.

2. Blurred mind blurred vision – The "Author of Confusion" and lies. Many are engaged in worldly self-help gurus, mystics, eastern meditation, and believing in a higher power but not through Jesus Christ, the (Messiah) the anointed one.

3. Following meditation and success gurus – Success gurus that have stolen biblical success principles and used them to deceive people into thinking they created them, and eastern world meditation practices, like transcendental meditation, etc.

4. Apostasy and disobedience will reign – This is so prevalent in today's world and many areas of life, from children to adults. *There will be an increase in this beginning in the year 2013... Hmm, watch and see!*

5. The unequally yoked factor – Viewed as unholy alliances or the conforming to worldly views, agendas through manipulation.

Here it is right here…

…that old serpent, called the Devil, and Satan, which deceiveth the whole world: … Revelation 12:9. Yes, this deception is everywhere. Do you believe that you are deceived? You know, scripture refers to it. Oh, the unbelievers of Jesus Christ and what the covenant Word of God says… They will say and continue to say that the Word of God contradicts itself. Attempting to obtain understanding with a carnal mindset, contradiction, and confusion is what they will experience. Can you see it? Can you see the deception? As you reflect back on what you have read, think about those elect deceived in this prophetic "Night Vision Revealed". I am sure they thought they were in right standing, but the manifested results proved otherwise. What position can you begin to place yourself in so that you are in the proper strategic position like those who had a first class ticket? As mentioned earlier the right preparation is a key factor in obtaining your ticket. Oh, standing in line does not matter because you can purchase one anytime, anywhere but there is a cost. Just remember, you cannot purchase it with your wealth, your works alone cannot purchase it, but granted onto you through obedience to His word, His love and by the grace of God! Unfortunately, not everyone will partake in it.

Reflection of Deception and Reflection of Truth

As I reflect on this night vision and transported from scene to scene, I realize that truth and deception was present simultaneously at all times. Oh yes, I have you thinking! You may be asking how so? How can truth and deception be present at all times in this night vision? The truth was present when I experienced the disagreement between my wife and myself. The deception is the thought of doing nothing wrong and not asking for forgiveness or repenting. The truth was numerous people "Caught Up" in this night vision… The deception of the enemy caused many to miss the "Caught Up" flight. Can you put yourself in the shoes of one of those who were in right standing or not in right standing? Which position will you be in when the occurrence of it takes place? Are the last two statements challenging to grasp? At the appointed time, all will witness it and see it. Now, take heed to the warning signs mentioned above, (The Enemy Has Deceived You).

The Night Vision Revealed Closure

As this night vision closes, I pray that you believe and receive this true prophetic night vision, and that it has opened your eyes to what is to come in the very near future. I ask that you take heed to and grasp hold to God's prophetic time clock and agenda because it is truly that. Do not make the mistake that I made in the beginning of this night vision, as it is detrimental to your eternal home address. Just like in all things, there is a time for preparation, and time is such a precious commodity, so do not waste it and say I will do it tomorrow when you can do it now. The (do it now) is, ask the Lord to be your savior right now if you have not done so, and get in right standing with the Lord thy God. Please remember that someone had to share and tell this prophetic night vision, and that is why I was not only an observer but a participant as well. Remember this… *Watch therefore [give strict attention, be cautious and active], for you do not know in what kind of a day [whether a near or remote one] your Lord is coming.* Matthew 24:42 AMP

Would you like to know more?

[CHAPTER 12]
The Seals of God In-Depth Revelation

MENTIONED EARLIER IN CHAPTER 5 of this book you briefly read about the (The Seal of God). As you move forward within the realm of this prophetic night vision, I will take you deeper into the seven seals of God, so that you get understanding and revelation. I do not desire for you to remain ignorant (not knowing), and I believe the Lord has already said the same thing. It says… ("*But if any man be ignorant, let him be ignorant*". First Corinthians 14:38) of the things that are prophesied for the end of the Church age. Therefore, it is very important that I share this with those who will believe and receive through their faith of the revelation that came to me through this night vision. Before we dive into the seals, the "Book of Revelation" is broken down into three parts.

As mentioned earlier, they are…

1. Past: The "things which" you have seen

2. Present: The "things which" are

3. Future: The "things which" shall be hereafter

So what are the seals that the "Book of Revelation" is referring too? What role do they play in the "End-Of-The-Church-Age" and God's prophetic agenda and time clock? How do they effect what will take place in heaven and on the earth? What does it mean to humanity, salvation and the eternal outcome? First, we must understand that the English title "Revelation" comes from the first word of the book in Greek. The word is "*apokalypsis*", which means, "the unveiling of something previously unrevealed." Here it is, there is a scroll with seven "seals", by blasts from seven "trumpets", and by the wrath of God poured out from seven "bowls" or "vials", and they all play a significant role in the prophetic program of Jesus Christ and God. They flow from one to another in a series of actions brought forth by the angels, instructed by the Lord thy God and seen by John the Apostle in a vision. If you have not noticed, they flow in three's. This can go further; there are seven Churches (1:11), seven candlesticks (1:13), seven stars (1:16), seven letters (2:1-3:22), seven Spirits (4:5), seven seals (5:1), seven trumpets (8:2), seven thunders (10:3), seven heads (12:3; 13:1), seven angels (15:6), seven bowls or vials, (15:7), seven mountains (17:9), and seven blessings (1:3; 14:13; 16:15; 19:9; 20:6; 22:7, 14). The number seven is very prominent in the Book of Revelation… Can you see how scripture confirms it all? The number seven represents the completeness and perfection.

In addition to this we must not forget the number four (4:6; 6:1-8; 9:14) and the number twelve (7:4-8; 21:12, 14; 22:2) also appear to have special significance. I hope that all readers of this book is ready for what I am about to share. If you think it has already "wet your noodle", you have not read anything yet. I am now about to wet your noodle further; and how "Caught Up Night Vision Revealed" flows with the "Book of Revelation", the "Book of Daniel", and the "Book of Isaiah" and the connection each one has. Here is a little hint; the connection established itself in the beginning of this prophetic night vision. If you did not catch it, it is OK. If you desire too continue reading, I recommend that you do, in order to obtain more understanding and revelation…

Would you like to know more?

It Begins Again

The Outline: "The Revelation and unveiling of Jesus Christ", He is coming…

1. PAST: The things which you have seen… - Revelation Chapter 1: Reveals the revelation and the coming of our Lord Jesus Christ.

2. PRESENT: The things which are… - Revelation Chapter 2 & 3: Reveals the special messages sent to the seven Churches, located in Asia.

3. FUTURE: The things which shall be hereafter… - Revelation Chapter 4: …a door was opened in heaven: … an opportunity to see a glimpse of heaven and see the worship of the One "who sits on the throne."

   Revelation Chapter 5: The seal book with the authority of God, given to the Lamb of God, Jesus Christ worthy to open the scroll, stood in the midst of the throne…

   Revelation Chapter 6: The seals revealed… The Lamb of God (Jesus Christ) looses the seals; which marks the beginning of the tribulation…

   Revelation Chapter 7: The Lord's special servants (144,000) must be "sealed" before the judgments begin…

Revelation Chapter 8 & 9: Begins where chapter 6 ended… Within the seventh seal contains the seven trumpets, and describes the two woes – one and two. What are the woes (grief, anguish or affliction)?

- Woe 1: The fifth trumpet brings a five-month period of torment on the unbelievers of the earth. However, known as the "bottomless pit"

- Woe 2: the sixth trumpet results in the death of a "third" of the surviving unbelievers on the earth. Yes, "one third" of the population of the world killed by demons, and this will unfold at the river Euphrates…

Revelation Chapter 10: The angel and the little book - The lease has ended and this is most likely the "title deed" to the earth. It symbolizes Christ's right to posses and rules the earth. (cf. Jeremiah 32:10, 11)

Revelation Chapter 11: The two witnesses… The measuring of the temple of God and the rebuilding of it begins.

Revelation Chapter 12 - 14: Explanatory prophecies, that describes some of the major personages and movements, which take place during the Tribulation period.

Revelation Chapter 15: The preparation for the seven vials – The wrath of God, began with seven seals in (chapter 6), and will be finished with the seven last plagues, which are the seven vials (vs. 7). This is the introduction of these last plagues.

Revelation Chapter 16: Now, the vials of the wrath of God, it represents the climax of God's punishment of sinners during the

Tribulation period. Unfortunately, no repentance is invited or shown.

Revelation Chapter 17 & 18: Here the scene is set, it depicts the judgment of God on a system (a false religious system), empire, or city called Babylon the Great. The "*great whore*", named "BABYLON THE GREAT". Here it is… Babylon the harlot is the "MOTHER OF HARLOTS AND ABOMINATIONS OF THE EARTH". It is interesting how God uses a woman to symbolize a Church. How does (God) accomplish this? Since you are reading this book, I am almost certain that you are wondering and asking how! He (God) uses a virgin (pure) to symbolize His true Church (bride) and a harlot to symbolize the false compromised Church of the end time.

Revelation Chapter 19 & 20: Brings the beginning of the climax of the Book of Revelation: The return of Jesus Christ to establish His millennial kingdom, and the marriage supper of the lamb preparation. It escalates into the *armies* of the *beast*, and of the kings of the east, and all the earth will gather in Palestine at (Armageddon). The attempt is to prevent the return, and the kingdom of Christ. Satan is finally arrested, and bound for a thousand years.

Revelation Chapter 21: John a servant of Christ, exiled by the Roman emperor Domitian to the island of (Patmos) wrote down what he saw in his visions. John provides a description of the eternal state. He saw "*the first heaven and the first earth*", replaced by a "*new heaven and new earth*".

Revelation Chapter 22: This final chapter of Revelation summarizes the prophetic end-time agenda of the entire book, and all of what will take place.

Now that the outline of all twenty-two chapters are explained, it is now time to go to another level of understanding and revelation regarding God's seals. If you thought the outline said a lot, watch this…

Would you like to know more?

God's Seals Sequence of Prophetic Events

As we began to move into more understanding and revelation, that is based on the prophetic truth of the covenant Word of God. Let us begin to examine the first seal in chapter 6 as we look at the revealing of it by the Lamb of God and the other seals that follow.

THE CONQUEST: THE FIRST SEAL (A White Horse)

Book of Revelation 6: 1, 2 – [1]And I saw when the Lamb opened one of the seals, and I heard, as it were the noise of thunder, one of the four beasts saying, Come and see.

[2] And I saw, and behold a white horse: and he that sat on him had a bow; and a crown was given unto him: and he went forth conquering, and to conquer.

The First Seal – There are keywords that bring forth understanding and revelation in these two verses. They are…

1. We see that when the LAMB broke the "*first seal*", we see the first of four beast; a "*lion-like creature*" that cried with a loud voice of thunder. "*Come and see*". Note: The words "*and see*" are omitted in many manuscripts, and in the revised version, but clearly it is in verse-1 (KJV) of the scripture. It is very interesting here because John had no need to "*come and see*" for he was already there as the visions revealed to him. However, the command of "*come and see*" was to the "*rider*" of the "*white horse*".

2. When he appeared, John the Apostle says, and I saw, and behold a "*white horse*"; and he that sat on him holding a "*bow*"; and a "*crown was given unto him:*" and he went forth in the earth "*conquering*", and "*to conquer*".

The question is who is the "rider" upon the white horse? I believe we can conclude that it is not "Jesus Christ" because Christ is the "LAMB" who is holding the "Seven Sealed Book" and is breaking open the "first seal". Furthermore, the "rider" has a bow, but there is no mention of an arrow and he is not crowned at first, but a crown will be given to him later, the (4735, Stephanos – Strong's Concordance meaning, "That which surrounds, i.e. a crown or victor's crown", as a reward for his victories). I believe that the rider is the "Antichrist". The first seal initiates the worldwide conquest by the "false messiah" the "Antichrist". He will be the final Gentile world ruler. Unfortunately, he will be brilliant, irresistible and will amaze the world with his shrewdness; this will elevate him into a leadership role that will place him at the "Head of the Ten Federated Kingdoms" of the revived Roman Empire. This sets the scene for the "Christ" our champion who will appear on His "White Horse" in chapter 19:11 in the Book of Revelation to win the final battle of Armageddon.

WAR: THE SECOND SEAL (A Red Horse)

Book of Revelation 6: 3, 4 – [3] And when he had opened the second seal, I heard the second beast say, Come and see.

[4] And there went out another horse that was red: and power was given to him that sat thereon to take peace from the earth, and that they should kill one another: and there was given unto him a great sword.

The Second Seal – There are keywords that bring forth understanding and revelation in these two verses. They are…

1. When the *second seal* is broken, John the Apostle heard the second beast, or a "*calf-like living creature*" say, "*Come and see*", and a "*RED HORSE*" appeared and went forth into the earth, and this rider is now given a "*GREAT SWORD*", and who had power to "*take peace from the earth*", and cause men to "*kill one another*". The symbolism is very clear that "*red*", the color of the horse, is a symbol of "*BLOOD*", and the "*sword*" is a symbol of "*WAR*". This period, prophesied by Jesus Christ, when he said… "And ye shall hear of wars and rumors of wars": . . . "For nation shall rise against nation, and kingdom against kingdom": … Matthew 24:6-7

2. The *second seal* brings *war and a lack of peace*. The sword represents armed conflict.

Could this possibly be the attacks on Israel mentioned in the Book of Ezekiel in chapters 38 and 39? Some of you may be thinking that we are experiencing this right now, and we are to some extent, but rest assured that what these two scriptures (Rev. 6: 3, 4) describe is far worse than what we are witnessing at the current time. I want to make this perfectly clear at the time and writing of this book, the year is 2013, and we are currently not in the Tribulation period at this point and time. Other prophecies must come forth before we get too the Tribulation point and time on the prophetic time clock.

INFLATION and FAMINE: THE THIRD SEAL (A Black Horse)

Book of Revelation 6: 5, 6 – [5] And when he had opened the third seal, I heard the third beast say, Come and see. And I beheld, and lo a black horse; and he that sat on him had a pair of balances in his hand.

[6] And I heard a voice in the midst of the four beasts say, A measure of wheat for a penny, and three measures of barley for a penny; and see thou hurt not the oil and the wine.

The Third Seal – There are keywords that bring forth understanding and revelation in these two verses. They are…

1. Now that the *third seal* is broken, again, John the Apostle heard the third "*man-like living creature*" and it says… "*Come and see*" and a "*BLACK HORSE*" appeared and went forth into the earth, and this rider held in his hand a "*pair of balances*", and a voice came forth again from one

of the four beast say… "*A measure of wheat for a penny*", and "*three measures of barley for a penny*", and see thou "*hurt not*" the "*oil*" and the "*wine*".

2. I truly believe that the third seal symbolizes inflation and (famine – black horse), and the rider the "*Conserver of Food*". The "*balances*" or scales related to commerce and trade. The word "*penny*", better-transliterated "*denarius*", represented about one day's wages. The "*wheat and barley*" considered necessities of life. A "*measure*" (Gr. *choinix*) is about one quart. The price given is about 10 times what was normal. The command "*hurt not the oil and the wine*" may indicate a restriction on the effects of the famine that will be great in the early part of the Tribulation.

As we also expound on these two scriptures, it also appears that we are experiencing this right now, but again rest assured it would be for more worse, than what it is now. Now that we have expounded on the first three seals, can you now see God's prophetic agenda unfold? Can you see it? Can you see it?

Would you like to know more?

DEATH: THE FOURTH SEAL (A Pale Horse)

Book of Revelation 6: 7, 8 – [7] And when he had opened the fourth seal, I heard the voice of the fourth beast say, Come and see.

[8] And I looked, and behold a pale horse: and his name that sat on him was Death, and Hell followed with him. And power was given unto them over the fourth part of the earth, to kill with sword, and with hunger, and with death, and with the beasts of the earth.

The Fourth Seal – There are keywords that bring forth understanding and revelation in these two verses. They are…

1. Now we see that the *fourth seal* is broken, John the Apostle heard the fourth beast "*eagle-like living creature*" says… "*Come and see*" and a "*PALE HORSE*" appeared and went forth into the earth. The color of the pale horse appears "corps like" in color.

2. The "*rider*" upon this "*PALE HORSE*" called "*DEATH*", and "HELL" followed with him.

This pale rider brings *death* to *one-fourth* of the population *of the earth*, through war, famine, and pestilence. Here it is right here… *Death* takes lives, and *Hell* (Hades) holds them for judgment. The destruction and loss of human life is extremely great from the fourth seal. When we examine the "*SWORD*", "*HUNGER*", "*DEATH*", and the "*BEASTS OF THE EARTH*", they derive from the prophecy, prophesied called the "*FOUR SORE JUDGMENTS*" found in the Book of Ezekiel 14:21 that are to come upon Jerusalem. This of course will be devastating and awful days and times, but the "Church" will not be a partaker of this because it will be "caught up" as promised by the Word of God. At this point and time you think that repentance and calling on the Lord thy God is at hand, but instead they will run to hide in the mountains and rocks to hide from the face of Him (God), and what is to come, "*The great day of the wrath*". It is the day of the Lord, the predicted time of God's judgment of the earth and its inhabitants. As you can see, missing the first class flight, the "catching away" will be costly to many left behind to endure the very troubling times prophesied by God and the prophets.

MARTYRDOM: THE FIFTH SEAL (The Mighty Slain Souls)

Book of Revelation 6: 9-11 – [9] And when he had opened the fifth seal, I saw under the altar the souls of them that were slain for the word of God, and for the testimony which they held:

> [10] And they cried with a loud voice, saying, How long, O Lord, holy and true, dost thou not judge and avenge our blood on them that dwell on the earth?
>
> [11] And white robes were given unto every one of them; and it was said unto them, that they should rest yet for a little season, until their fellow servants also and their brethren, that should be killed as they were, should be fulfilled.

The Fifth Seal – There are keywords that bring forth understanding and revelation in these three verses. They are…

1. Again, as the *fifth seal* is opened, revealed to John the Apostle in his continuing vision was a "*Sacrificial Alter*", which corresponds to the "*Burnt Offering Altar*", the "*SOULS*" of them that were slain for their belief in the "*Word of God*", but not just their belief but for their "*testimony*" of Christ. Call them (Martyrdom of Tribulation Saints) throughout the world. They will come to faith in Christ following the "rapture or catching away". Numerous souls killed by satanic oppression.

2. Those turning towards Christ during this Tribulation period will experience tremendous persecution. Jesus Christ said in (Matthew 24:9-14), emphasizes placed on verse-14… "*And this gospel of the kingdom shall be preached in all the*

world for a witness unto all nations; and then shall the end come". However when we look at Acts 20:24, we can clearly see that this is taking place right NOW! Due to the fact that we are under the grace of God.

3. These souls were sacrifices, yes martyrs. Their "*white robes*" depict their righteous standing before God. Here it is right here… these souls were not the Martyrs of the Christian Church, because they were resurrected and "caught up" with the Church. These Martyrs' are those killed for the "Word of God" and their testimony after the Church is "caught up".

Many more saints will end up as martyrs as well since there is more of the Tribulation to come forth on the earth during this time.

NATURAL DISASTERS: THE SIXTH SEAL (Changes in the Heavens and Earth)

Book of Revelation 6: 12-17 – [12] And I beheld when he had opened the sixth seal, and, lo, there was a great earthquake; and the sun became black as sackcloth of hair, and the moon became as blood;

[13]And the stars of heaven fell unto the earth, even as a fig tree casteth her untimely figs, when she is shaken of a mighty wind.

[14]And the heaven departed as a scroll when it is rolled together; and every mountain and island were moved out of their places.

[15]And the kings of the earth, and the great men, and the rich men, and the chief captains, and the mighty men, and every bondman, and every free man, hid themselves in the dens and in the rocks of the mountains;

[16] And said to the mountains and rocks, Fall on us, and hide us from the face of him that sitteth on the throne, and from the wrath of the Lamb:

[17] For the great day of his wrath is come; and who shall be able to stand?

The Sixth Seal – There are keywords that bring forth understanding and revelation in these six verses. They are…

1. The *sixth seal* is different; it is special because it will bring forth natural disasters of various kinds according to (Matthew 24:7-9). When John the Apostle saw the *sixth seal* opened, a *great earthquake* sprang forth, as the earth

and the heavenly bodies will go into great convulsions or "travail pangs". Joel 2:30, 31 predicts many of these judgments in nature as signs of the day of the Lord.

A shaking like no other comes forth. Here it is right here…

- "**GREAT EARTHQUAKE**"… the earth will go into convulsions
- "**SUN BECAME BLACK AS SACKCLOTH OF HAIR**"… will not shine its great light (obscured)
- "**MOON BECAME AS BLOOD**"… the light of this heavenly body is no longer bright and will not shine
- "**STARS OF HEAVEN FELL UNTO THE EARTH**"… meteors and shooting stars
- "**HEAVEN DEPARTED AS A SCROLL**"… the sky split apart
- "**EVERY MOUNTAIN AND ISLAND WERE MOVED OUT OF THEIR PLACE**"… a geographical shifting and rearranging of land mass
- "**KINGS OF THE EARTH etc**"… great fear will fall upon all humankind of the earth
- "**GREAT DAY OF HIS WRATH**"… the day of the Lord "is come – means God's Day of Judgment is here". It has finally arrived, having begun with the first six seals

This is a number of things that will take place. These were prophesied events foretold by the prophets and by Jesus Christ himself. There will be a shaking in the earth and in heaven like no other. Here is something that will again wet your noodle. There was a time in history that the prophet Zechariah 14:1-7 spoke about, "clear nor dark" in verse-6 or (there will be no light, the lights will diminish). Now, let us backup to the Book of Isaiah 13:9, 10 and Isaiah 34:4, as this corresponds to and relates to the "stars of heaven" of the "*sixth seal*". Because of these first *six seal* judgments, many unbelievers of Jesus Christ will most likely want to die and or hide from God, but that will not be the case. *The great day of the wrath* is the day of the Lord, the predicted time of God's judgment of the earth and its inhabitants (cf. Joel 1:15; 2:1, 11, 31). The day or wrath contrasted to the present "day of grace". "*Is come*", means God's day-of-judgment "is here" – it has finally arrived, having begun with the first *six seals*.

Would you like to know more?

We are now entering into the seventh seal, but before I expound on it, we must get some additional understanding of the 144,000 sealed. You see, God's prophetic clock continues to tick tock, tick tock, and fulfill many special manifested events. Here it is… There is a frame of time called the "God time interval" – *the system of those sequential relations that any event has to any other, as past, present, or future; indefinite and continuous duration regarded as that in which events succeed one another.* In the Book of Revelation 7:1-8 it spells out what must occur, and not to occur on the earth according to the Lord thy God. This special event has to take place before the opening of the *seventh seal.* A stamp of approval, granted onto the 144,000 children of Israel, sealed in their foreheads from God. This supernatural power granted unto them during this time will not bow to the knee of the Antichrist. Oh, what Glory!

In (verse 1) of the scriptures, we see God's program of *grace and salvation* during the period of judgment. The "*winds*" depict God's judgment of the earth, and the "*four angels*" are restraining agents who hold back the judgment until God's special "*servants*" are "*sealed*" and we see this in (verse 3). The seal shows ownership and security, as a king's signet ring which is used to authenticate and protect official documents. As we see in (verse 4) the 144,000 all Israelites from the 12 tribes (12 times 12,000), this is *the seed of Abraham.* This number may be taken literally or figuratively of a national conversion. All 12 tribes returned from exile, and there was always a remnant from the entire nation in Israel (cf. 2 Chronicles 30:1-10, 25, 26; Matthew 10:5, 6; Acts 26:7). The promise of future restoration given to all 12 tribes (cf. Isaiah 11:11-13; Ezekiel 37:15-28). This is truly prophetic! There are no “lost tribes”. Here it is… In the list of tribes, we see Joseph stands for Ephraim, and Dan or (Danites) is missing, possibly because it was the first tribe to go into idolatry and apostasy (cf. Judges 18). Here it is again… The 144,000 will apparently be converted and commissioned to be a light to the Gentiles during the Tribulation period.

A HUSH IN HEAVEN: THE SEVENTH SEAL (A Time of Silence)

Book of Revelation 8: 1-5 – [1]And when he had opened the seventh seal, there was silence in heaven about the space of half an hour.

[2]And I saw the seven angels which stood before God; and to them were given seven trumpets.

[3] And another angel came and stood at the altar, having a golden censer; and there was given unto him much incense, that he should offer it with the prayers of all saints upon the golden altar which was before the throne.

[4]And the smoke of the incense, which came with the prayers of the saints, ascended up before God out of the angel's hand.

[5] And the angel took the censer, and filled it with fire of the altar, and cast it into the earth: and there were voices, and thunderings, and lightnings, and an earthquake.

The Seventh Seal – There are keywords that bring forth understanding and revelation in these five verses. They are…

1. First, chapter 8 begins where chapter 6 ends. The *seventh seal* flows into and contains the *seven trumpets*. Now the word "*silence*" in verse-1 indicates the beginning of something, and that something is further series of judgments. The period is in a time span, a *space of half an hour*. We can call this calmness before the fury of the actual storm.

2. In verse-2, John the Apostle sees in his continued vision, *seven angels*, and they stood before God, poised and ready because God personally gave each of the seven angels, *seven trumpets*. These trumpets are very symbolic because of what the trumpet represents…

    - Trumpets are used as a call to war
    - Trumpets are used to worship
    - Trumpets are used for the convocation (assembly) of the people
    - Trumpets are used to proclaim festivals
    - Trumpets are used for the year of Jubilee
    - Trumpets are used for the feast of tabernacles
    - Trumpets will be used in God's judgments

The following scriptures verify the various usage of the trumpets use… (Exodus 19:16. Amos 3:6. Joshua 6:13-16. Zephaniah 1:14-16). You can be sure that the seven angels will take up strategic positions to sound their trumpet at the appointed time.

3. Before this takes place, John the Apostle sees another angel holding something special; it is a *golden censer*; and *incense*. The incense is often an illustration of prayer (cf. 5:8). I believe the Trumpet judgments just may be God's response to the *prayer of the saints* in (6:10), the saints of

the Tribulation period – and a cry for revenge against the enemies of Jesus Christ.

4. The *golden censer*, filled with "*Fire of the Alter*" from heaven, thrown into the earth, which represents the coming of judgment on the earth.

5. Christ will use angels to administer the trumpets. The blast of each "*trumpet*" not only breaks the silence of heaven, it also symbolizes the execution of God's judgment.

Would you like to know more?

The Transition from Seals to Trumpets

As we now transition from the seven seals to the seven trumpets, God's judgment continues aggressively on and in the earth. Each sound of the trumpet represents the "God judgment events" in a series of seven, bringing catastrophic results in the earth and to humankind.

THE HEARING OF IT: THE SEVEN TRUMPETS (Prepared too sound)

Book of Revelation 8: 6-13 – 6And the seven angels which had the seven trumpets prepared themselves to sound.

7 The first angel sounded, and there followed hail and fire mingled with blood, and they were cast upon the earth: and the third part of trees was burnt up, and all green grass was burnt up.

8 And the second angel sounded, and as it were a great mountain burning with fire was cast into the sea: and the third part of the sea became blood;

9 And the third part of the creatures which were in the sea, and had life, died; and the third part of the ships were destroyed.

10And the third angel sounded, and there fell a great star from heaven, burning as it were a lamp, and it fell upon the third part of the rivers, and upon the fountains of waters;

[11]And the name of the star is called Wormwood: and the third part of the waters became wormwood; and many men died of the waters, because they were made bitter.

[12] And the fourth angel sounded, and the third part of the sun was smitten, and the third part of the moon, and the third part of the stars; so as the third part of them was darkened, and the day shone not for a third part of it, and the night likewise.

[13] And I beheld, and heard an angel flying through the midst of heaven, saying with a loud voice, Woe, woe, woe, to the inhabiters of the earth by reason of the other voices of the trumpet of the three angels, which are yet to sound!

The Seven Trumpets – There are keywords that bring forth understanding and revelation in these seven verses. They are…

John the Apostle continues to watch his prophetic vision, as he sees the angels pour out the plagues by the sound of the trumpets… These plagues have happen before and will happen again…

1. The "*first angel sounded*" its trumpet, and brings forth literal fire and hail, and causes the destruction of most of the vegetation on the earth. From this, famine and a lack of oxygen fall on the earth.

2. The "*second angel sounded*" its trumpet, and turns a third of the sea into blood, and a third of the sea creatures and ships are destroyed. Because of this, their will be a shortage of rain, and fresh water on the land. This will affect International commerce and distribution of food and resources.

3. The "*third angel sounded*" its trumpet, and makes a third of all fresh water bitter, resulting in widespread thirst and death. The star called "*wormwood*" (Gr. *apsinthos*, lit. "*Undrinkable*"), a bitter herb (cf. Proverbs 5:4) that will make the water of the earth unfit for human consumption.

4. The "*fourth angel sounded*" its trumpet, takes away a *third* of the light from the heavens during both *day* and *night*. The light arriving from the *sun,* the *stars*, and *moon* reduced significantly. This will lead to fear on the earth, it will also affect many other things on the earth, such as crop production and the quality of life (cf. Matthew 24:29; Luke 21:25). The last three trumpets (*remaining blast about*) will be especially severe, as announced by an angel in verse-13 of the Book of Revelation, and it is "*Woe, woe, woe*"; directed towards the *inhabitants of the earth*, that is the unbelievers still alive on earth. Note: The Revised Version, and many Manuscripts substitute "**Eagle**" for "**Angel**", but that does not affect the meaning.

Transitioning into the trumpets Chapter 9:

THE HEARING OF IT: THE SEVEN TRUMPETS (continues)...

Book of Revelation 9: 1-21 – Read and meditate on these scriptures.

The Seventh Trumpets – There are keywords that bring forth understanding and revelation in these twenty-one verses. They are…

Rev. 9:1-3

5. The "*fifth angel sounded*" its trumpet, that begins the first two woes – trumpets *five* and *six*.

    - The *fifth trumpet* brings forth a five-month period of torment on the unbelievers of the earth

    - A *star* falls from heaven. What is this star? Whom does this star represent? Could this star be an angel of God (cf. 1:20; 20:1) or Satan, (the one who has authority over the pit (cf. v. 11; Isaiah 14:12; Luke 10:18)?

Illustration: The Underworld or Bottomless Pit

View on the next page | Public Domain Usage

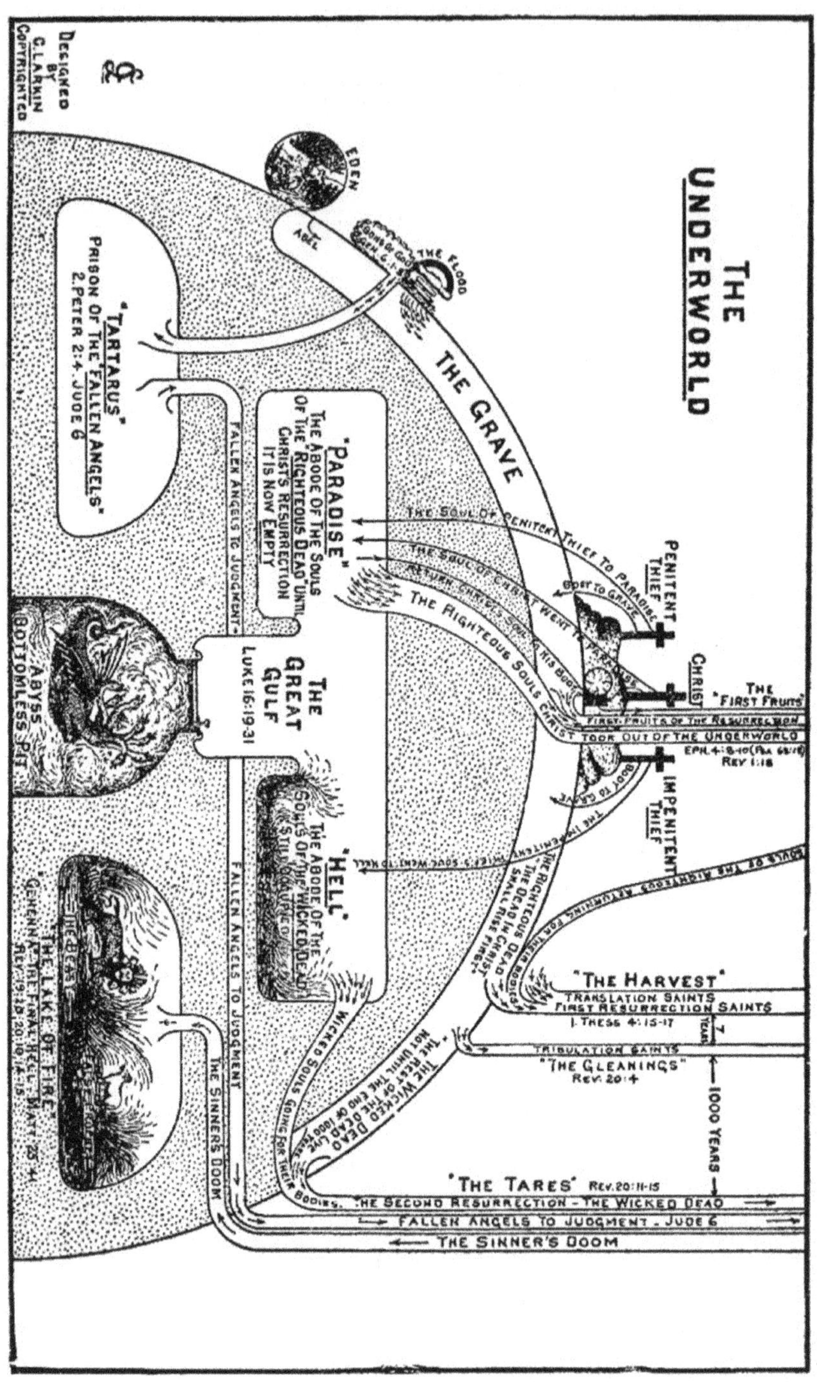
THE UNDERWORLD
DESIGNED BY C. LARKIN COPYRIGHTED
EDEN
ABEL
THE FLOOD
THE GRAVE
"TARTARUS"
PRISON OF THE "FALLEN ANGELS"
2.PETER 2:4. JUDE 6
"PARADISE"
THE ABODE OF THE SOULS OF THE "RIGHTEOUS DEAD" UNTIL CHRIST'S RESURRECTION
IT IS NOW EMPTY
THE GREAT GULF
LUKE 16:19-31
ABYSS
BOTTOMLESS PIT
"HELL"
THE ABODE OF THE SOULS OF THE "WICKED DEAD"
"THE LAKE OF FIRE"
GEHENNA - THE FINAL HELL
PENITENT THIEF
CHRIST
IMPENITENT THIEF
THE "FIRST FRUITS"
CHRIST TOOK OUT OF THE UNDERWORLD
"THE HARVEST"
TRANSLATION SAINTS
FIRST RESURRECTION SAINTS
I. THESS 4:15-17
TRIBULATION SAINTS
"THE GLEANINGS"
REV. 20:4
1000 YEARS
"THE TARES" REV. 20:11-15
THE SECOND RESURRECTION - THE WICKED DEAD
FALLEN ANGELS TO JUDGMENT . JUDE 6
THE SINNER'S DOOM

- The *bottomless pit* is the Abyss, the abode (*residence*) of evil spirits or demons.

The *key* represents authority.

Illustration: Many will not believe this. It begins with (if)

If you have trouble believing in God or God could ever make a hell, remember it was prepared for the Devil and his fallen angels. See (Matthew 25:41).

Application: Hell does exist
Those who go to "*hell*" are in essence choosing to spend eternity with Satan rather than with Christ. If you do not believe this, because this is what the Word of God says… then die and find out!

First Reference: Read
Genesis 2:17
Primary Reference: Read
Revelation 9:1-12; cf. Luke 16:23-25

The *smoke* from the "*pit*" indicates *fires* below. Out of the smoke come (locust that symbols destruction and demons), and like *scorpions*, they can hurt people.

Rev. 9:4-6

No harm comes to the vegetation of the earth, but only to *men (humanity)* who do not belong to God. At this point, the locust like creatures cannot *kill* anyone for five months, but they *torment* those that do not have the seal of God stamped on their foreheads or in their right hands.

Rev. 9:7-10

They take on a physical form in order to manifest their destruction and torment. The *horses* show their warlike character. Their *crown* depicts them as conquerors. Their *human* faces show intelligence. Their *feminine* hair perhaps makes them seductive and attractive. The *teeth of lions* shows, them to be destructive and hurtful. Their *breastplates of iron* make them indestructible. Their *wings* symbolize swiftness. The *stings* of their *tails* give them the *power* to *hurt*. Fortunately, for humankind they will only endure this for five months. Unfortunately, the next woe (judgment) is WORSE!

Rev. 9:11, 12

These demons had a *ruler* or a *king* over them and apparently, it was Satan, given temporary authority over the Abyss. Satan known in the Hebrew tongue as *Abaddon* or "Destruction", but in the Greek tongue, its equivalent is Apollyon, meaning "Destroyer". However, *two* more *woes* are still to come. As the end approaches, the intensity and severity of the trumpet judgments increase dramatically. I know these things are horrible, but God's prophetic word will "come to pass".

As John the Apostle continues his vision he again hears a "*voice from the four horns of the golden alter which is before God*"…

Rev. 9:13-15

6. The "*sixth angel sounded*" its trumpet, and it brings forth the results in the death of a *third* of the surviving unbelievers on the earth. As we look at the *four angels*, they are fallen angels or demons temporarily *bound (prisoner)* by God. Prepared and waiting at the "river Euphrates". Can you see that God is still in control? Their purpose is for killing a "*third*" of the population of the world. Wow; what a horrific event that is on the future horizon for the End-Of-The-Church-Age and those left behind to endure this. These fallen angels appear to be in charge of a *horde* (a large group or multitude) of demonic-horsemen who will carry out this massacre. One could possibly place this event in a category of a (World War). However, this is not a conventional war event, but a manifested demonic unconventional war event.

Rev. 9:16-19

John the Apostle now *heard* the *number* of the "*horse-men*": It is *200,000,000*- literally, "*two myriads of myriads*", but the majority of manuscripts read "a myriad of myriads" or 100,000,000 (cf. 5:11; Psalm 68:17; Daniel 7:10 pertaining to the heavenly Sanhedrin, and not the latter). – I believe (verse-16 and the number 200,000,000) is the accurate account of what John saw in his vision. These "*horse-men*" belong to Satan's army, and they were not like normal "*horse-men*" in the sense of what we see in the present, or what was of the past. They are unholy supernatural beings.

Now, again, here is what John the Apostle saw in the vision…

- The "*riders*" upon these horses had "*Breastplates* of *FIRE and fiery red*" with "*Jacinth – blue sulfur*, and *yellow burning sulfur*"…

- They also had "*brimstone*" to match the *breath* of the horses upon which they rode…

- The "*head of lions*" symbolize cruelty and destruction…

- The *fire*, *smoke*, and *brimstone* are three separate plagues, which kill a *third* of mankind… here it is right here, these demon riders do kill; because their *power* to kill is in their *mouth*, from which come the "*fire*", "*smoke*", and "*brimstone*"…

- The description of these demons continues, because their *tails* have *heads* like *serpents*, with the *power* to *hurt* people. Here it is right here, this "*sixth trumpet*", combined with the "*fourth seal*" (Rev. 6:8), reduces the earth's population to *one-half* its "Pre-Tribulation" level.

Unfortunately, during this "Tribulation" period, most of the surviving unbelievers will have most likely made up their minds concerning "*Christ*". Those who do not believe that, "…every knee shall bow… (Philippians 2:10)", and "…every tongue shall confess… (Philippians 2:11)", by choosing who will you serve are in for a big surprise!

Rev. 9:20, 21

Many will not believe written here, and that is a choice, one will have to make. However, during this time, many will refuse to repent, even under this terrible judgment.

Would you like to know more?

An Interval Where Time Continues To Come Out Of Him

There is a time interval between the sixth trumpet and the seventh trumpet. John the Apostle visions continues through (Rev. 10:1 – 11:14), apparently it relates to the time covered by the first six trumpets, and thus to the latter half of the tribulation which includes the third woe and the quickness of its coming in the earth. As we progress quickly to the "*seventh angel sounded*", a number of significant events continue to present itself.

The Angel and the Little Book – Read Revelation 10:1-11

John the Apostle sees in his vision another mighty angel descend from heaven…

- The "*mighty angel*" (*may be a strong angel*). This describes Christ Himself (*the Angel of the Lord*)… Read Ezekiel 1:26-28

Little Book:

- This "*little book*" could possibly be the "*seventh sealed book*" now open, and is most likely the *title deed*, the (document containing or constituting evidence of ownership) to the earth. It symbolizes Christ's right to possess and rule the earth

- The "*loud voice*" shows authority as well

- Their came "*seven thunders*" as uttered voices, that may be the seven bowl judgments still to come in (Rev. chapter 16)

- "*Seal*" up the things which the seven thunders uttered, since they will be described in detail later – Read Daniel 12:9

- Their was a lifting of the "*hand*" signifying taking an oath – Read Daniel 12:7

- With the sound of the "*seventh angel sounded*" in (Rev. 11:15), the present *mystery form of the kingdom* will be over and what God promised to the *prophets* will finally be completed

I want to bring something to everyone's attention in (verses 8-10 of Rev. Chapter 10). The angel gave John one very specific instruction and it was…

1. John the Apostle instructions, to *eat* the *little book* and when he does, it becomes…

    - *Sweet* in his mouth and *bitter* in his *belly*

This "*little book*", is probably the same "*book*" that Daniel was told to "*seal up*" in the Book of Daniel 12:4, 9, could this be true? That "book" contained hidden things, secret things not revealed until the "*time of the end*" according to the Word of God, and not the "*end of time*" but the possibility of the "*end*" of the "times of the gentiles". When one examines this, it correlates with the last half of Daniel's "seventieth week" and therefore with "The Great Tribulation Period" and the instructions that the angel gave John appears too come into view and alignment with the return of Christ to the earth to setup His "*Millennial Kingdom*".

The second instruction John the Apostle received from the angel in verse 11 of Rev. Chapter 10:

2. John the Apostle instructions, is to prophesy again to…

    - Prophesy too many people…

    - Prophesy too nations, and in tongues, and to kings… (*This is a high level of prophetic utterances*)

As we move to the next chapter and closer to the *seventh angel sounded*, we also get closer to a new beginning.

Would you like to know more?

The Power of the Two Witnesses – Read Revelation 11:1-14

John the Apostle continues to receive instructions from the same angel that handed him the "*little book*" to seal it up and to eat it. Pay close attention to chapter 11 of (Rev.) because it is very significant in what it represents by the number (seven, its completion).

There are keywords that bring forth understanding and revelation in these fourteen verses. They are…

Rev. 11:1, 2

- The angel instructed (John the Apostle) to "*measure the Temple of God*". This temple is most likely the prophesied rebuilt millennial temple in Jerusalem (cf. Ezekiel Chapters 40 -42), and not the temple of Herod, because the destruction of the (temple of Herod) was by Roman troops under Titus during the Siege of Jerusalem in 70 AD. Note: It is apparent that there will be a temple at Jerusalem during the reign of the Antichrist, for he shall "*…sitteth in the temple of God... Second Thess. 2:3, 4*", and proclaim himself God. This parallels the "abomination of desolation" prophesied by Jesus Christ and the prophet Daniel in (Matt. 24:15; cf. Dan. 9:27; 11:31; 12:11)

- The outer *court* represents the control of Jerusalem and Israel by Gentiles during the last half of the Tribulation period

- The *holy city* is the earthly Jerusalem, see (cf. Dan. 9:24; 11:45; Zech. 13:8, 9; 14:2)

- The *forty and two months* show that Jerusalem will be under Gentile control for three-and-a-half years, most likely the last half of the seven-year Tribulation period, see (cf. Dan. 9:24-27, this is where the Great Tribulation is seen as the Seventieth Week or seven-year period in God's *postexilic (*occurring*) prophetic agenda* of Israel)

Rev. 11:3, 4

Power, given to the *two witnesses* (are two men, prophets of God), clothe in sackcloth they will *prophesy* and or preach in Israel for a certain number of days (1,260) or (three-and-a half years – 42 months), this is based on prophetical years of 360 days each. Most likely, this takes place during the last half of the Tribulation period. So the question is who are the two witnesses?

1. First, they are men, and not systems, they are empowered with supernatural power from God

2. Secondly, they bear similarities to John the Baptist (John 1:21 – John the Baptist, who appears in the likeness of Elijah ("in the spirit and power of Elijah"). In addition to this the ultimate fulfillment of the promised return of Prophet Elijah, (power to shut up the heavens, *not be dew nor rain* for a time frame of three years and six months – cf. First Kings 17:1; Luke 4:24; James 5:17). However, there was a *prophetic announcement* and a *prophetic decree* made by Malachi in (Malachi 4:5, 6 – John the Baptist, who appears in the likeness of Elijah). Verse 4 is the announcement and verse 5 is the decree

These two witnesses are channels of God's power and message to Israel during the Tribulation period. Oh, what glory this will be!

Rev. 11:5, 6

- They will perform miracles… The Word of God says these "two witnesses" have power…

    1. To "*shut heaven*", and that it "*rain not*" in the days of their prophecy. Does this sound familiar too you?

    2. They will have power over "*waters to turn them to blood*", and to smite the earth with "*all plagues*", as often as they will. Does this sound familiar too you?

If this does not sound familiar too you, then here it is… There miracles are similar to Moses (cf. Ex. 7:14-20; 8:12) and Elijah (First Kings 17:1; Second Kings 1:10-12; Luke 4:25; James 5:17)

- They are divinely protected from harm for three-and-a-half years

- There purpose, too authenticate their divine message

- Their message will be twofold (1) Jesus is the Lamb of God (Savior); and (2) Jesus is the King (Ruler). Listen up Israel, humanity, the King is coming to setup His kingdom, repentance is at hand

Rev. 11:7-10

- The *beast* ascends from the *bottomless pit*, the same as the "*beast*" from the sea in Rev 13:1; the *Antichrist* or *false prophet*

- At the end of the three-and-a-half years of preaching the two witnesses are finally killed by the beast in the *great city* identified as the place where our Lord was crucified (ref. to Jerusalem, at this time under the Antichrist's control. As such called (*Sodom* – referring to uncleanness and immorality & *Egypt* – depicting oppression and bondage)

- Bodies not buried

- The unbelievers of *the earth*, who have submitted to the authority of the beast, will *rejoice* because they despise the plagues and the message of the *two prophets* (cf. First Kings 18:17)

Rev. 11:11-14

- Here is the miracle and the power of God displayed. The two witnesses are brought back to *life*, and then taken up to *heaven…* here is the relation in this time interval, it took place in (*three-and-a-half days, and it is during the three-and-a-half years Tribulation period*)

- Their *enemies* react in *fear*, and their resurrection is incontrovertible (*incapable of being contradicted or disputed; undeniable*) proof that their message is true that Jesus is God and Messiah

- A mighty *earthquake* will kill *seven thousand men*, and many repented and gave *glory to God*

As chapter 11 ends, the *third woe* is to come quickly and includes the "vials" and all the other judgments in the Book of Revelation. In other words it is continuous, the seventh trumpet, which *comes* next beginning in (v. 15), because of the time interval between the 2nd and 3rd woe. The third woe mentioned now marks the finishing of God's judgment on sin; it occupies the book of Revelation through the 19th chapter, when Christ's Kingdom is established on earth, and now…

Rev. 11:15-19

7. The "*seventh angel sounded*" and the Lord sat down at the closing table poised and ready to take possession of the *title deed* (millennial kingdom) established permanently. This last trumpet of the angel flows into the vials and bowls in the beginning of (Rev. Chapter 16:1) or continued judgments. The overthrown of the kingdoms of this world by the coming kingdom of Christ, (cf. 19:11-21; Dan, 2:34, 35, 44) who will reign forever and ever. Here is your proof, read (cf. Dan. 7:13, 14, 27)

Before we accelerate to the vials/bowls, which are chapters (12-14 recommended reading) of the Book of Revelation, John the Apostle continues to receive very vivid visions. These chapters are explanatory prophecies that describe some of the major movements in the latter half of the Tribulation period.

Chapter 12:

1. The *woman* represents Israel, and her *child* is Christ…

2. The *sun* depicts her as God's chosen nation…

3. The *moon under her feet* alludes to God's promise of dominion…

4. The *crown of twelve stars* pictures royalty and relates to the 12 tribes of Israel…

5. The *birth* pains refer to the period before the birth of Christ…

As one reads the rest of chapter 12, ask the Lord for true understanding and revelation… Can you see the flow of it?

Chapter 13:

1. I believe the *sea* here represents the Gentile nations of the world, from which the *beast* comes… (cf. Matt. 24:5, 24; 1 John 2:18)

2. The description of the beast connects it to both the *dragon* and (Satan, 12:3)…

3. The *beast* has *horns* and *heads*…

4. The *beast* speaks *blasphemy* against God (cf. Rev. vv. 5, 6)…

5. The beast resemblances are to a *lion*, a *leopard*, and a *bear*, refers to the first three beasts in the vision of Daniel chapter 7 (representing the empires of Babylon, Medo-Persia, and Greece)…

6. **Special Note:** However, a fourth beast sprang forth that represents the Roman Empire...

As one reads the rest of chapter 13, ask the Lord for true understanding and revelation… Can you see the flow of it?

Chapter 14:

1. The *Lamb* is Christ, and *mount Zion* is the location of Jerusalem…

2. The 144,000 (12 times 12,000) are singing a new song of worship and redemption…

3. The everlasting gospel is the "Good News" that Christ will be victorious over the beast and the beast will be judged…

4. However, there are three parts: (1) *the hour of judgment to come* (2) *Babylon is fallen* (3) *those who worship the beast, punished forever…*

5. Unbelievers during the Tribulation will receive the *mark* of the *beast* and *worship* him… Sound familiar

As one reads the rest of chapter 14, ask the Lord for true understanding and revelation… Can you see the flow of it?

Would you like to know more?

Seven Plagues Cometh Too Destroy

We have seen the wrath of God begin with the seven seals in (chapter 6), and now finish with the *seven last plagues* which are seven vials (chapter 15:7). So now, another transition from the seven trumpets to the seven vials or bowls is at hand. Again, there is a flow and this is the third in the series of (seals, trumpets, and *vials*).

Transitioning into the vials Chapter 15 and 16:

As we now travel through chapter 15, John the Apostle saw a sign in heaven; this sign is of preparation, and an introduction of the seven golden vials. These vials represent the completion, and a pouring out of the accumulated wrath and or Tribulation judgments of what is too come forth. There are a few events and observations, that take place during this preparation time, and they are…

Rev. 15:1-4

1. John the Apostle saw in his vision, a "*sea of glass*", this is the same "*sea of glass*" that we saw before the throne in (chapter 4:6). At that time, it was unoccupied, but now occupied…

2. The *victory over the beast*, and over his "*image*" and over his "*mark*", and over the "*number of his name*" and they have harps, and they sing the "*song of Moses*" and the "*song of the Lamb*". They are the "harpers" of chapter 14:2, the 144,000 "sealed ones" that sing a new song of worship

and redemption won through faith "For Asking in the Heart" in Christ. *All nations* will come to and worship God in the millennial kingdom…

Rev. 15:5-8

The remaining part of Rev. Chapter 15 continues with the vision of John the Apostle and closes with…

1. The *seven angels* prepare to administer the last seven Tribulation judgments of Christ: the seven vials (cf. 16:1-17; 17:1; 21:9). These bowls are actually shallow "*bowls*" (Gr. *phiale*)…

    - The *bowls* contain the *full of the wrath of God.* The Lord thy God has the right to judge (Second Thess. 1:7-9) because He is the Eternal One; the Almighty

    - The *temple* represents the presence of God Himself

    - The *seven plagues* have to complete before anyone can *enter into the temple*

I will continue to say this, but many will not believe what I have written here, and that is OK, but I believe it and receive what the instruction manual says. The question is, do you? The prepping completed, and everything is in place, the last of His wrath begins…

Would you like to know more?

Signed Sealed & Completed

As mentioned throughout the many chapters of the Book of Revelation, John the Apostle continues in his vision from the Lord and says that he heard a great voice that came out of the temple. It is apparent that the Lord thy God instructed the seven angels too release the seven plagues from the vials. Here it is… the contents of these *vials (represent the climax of God's punishment of sinners during the Tribulation period)* are *literal*. These vial judgments are future events. Those unbelievers of Jesus Christ, who have accepted the "*mark of the beast*" will experience and see this "*literally fulfilled*", as I will describe here. What you the reader will discover is that four of the seven plagues actually happened before. Yes, they are simply repetitions of the "Plagues of Egypt", as revealed too you, as one continues to read… would you like to know more? Now, here is the proof!

Rev. 16:1-21 describes the seven plagues as the following…

1. First Vial: the first angel poured out his *vial* and it produces a painful (*sores* or *boils*) on all the followers of the *beast*… Note: This parallels sixth plague of Egypt (Ex. 9:8-11)

2. Second Vial: the second angel poured out his *vial* and turns the entire *sea* to *blood*, and the effect is death to all sea life. The *blood of a dead man*, coagulated (forms a clot) and rotting… Note: This parallels both the first plague on Egypt (Ex. 7:20, 21) and the second trumpet (Rev. 8:8, 9)

3. Third Vial: the third angel poured out his *vial* and turns all fresh *waters* to *blood*, and the effect is no pure drinking water left on earth… Note: Again, this parallels the first Egyptian plague, but also the third trumpet (Rev. 8:10, 11)

4. Fourth Vial: the fourth angel poured out his *vial* and scorched the earth with *fire* from the *sun*. Who are the ones scorched? The followers of the beast scorched…

5. Fifth Vial: the fifth angel poured out his *vial* and produces *darkness* on the *seat and kingdom of the beast…* Note: There are parallels with both the ninth plague of Egypt (Ex. 10:21-29) and the fourth trumpet (Rev. 8:12). With all the pain the followers of the beast were going through, they continued to disobey the Lord thy God and would not repent

6. Sixth Vial: the sixth angel poured out his *vial* and the results in the gathering of the armies of the *whole world* together in Palestine for the battle of "*Armageddon*" (from the Hebrew *Har Megiddon* – the Hill of Megiddo) at the river Euphrates. Note: There are parallels with the sixth trumpet (Rev. 9:13-21). The three unclean spirits are demons that truly support the activities of Satan, the *beast*, and the *false prophet...* Here is the prophecy, Jesus said… (*Behold, I come as a thief…* Rev. 16:15)

Now, the final Vial, "*It is done*":

7. Seventh Vial: the seventh angel poured out his *vial* and it destroys (the system), called the great city Babylon. With this vial, the return of Christ Himself and the judgments are

now finished. Furthermore, a great earthquake destroys the great city and *the cities of the nations*, and large *hail* fell upon the unbelievers of Jesus Christ. Note: There are parallels with the seventh plague of Egypt (Ex. 9:23-25). In closing of the seven vials, they are the last of the seven plagues (Rev. 15:6-8), it completes both the seventh trumpet (Rev. 11:15) and the seventh seal (Rev. 8:1)

Illustration: Seven Seals | Seven Trumpets | Seven Vials

View on the next page | Public Domain Usage

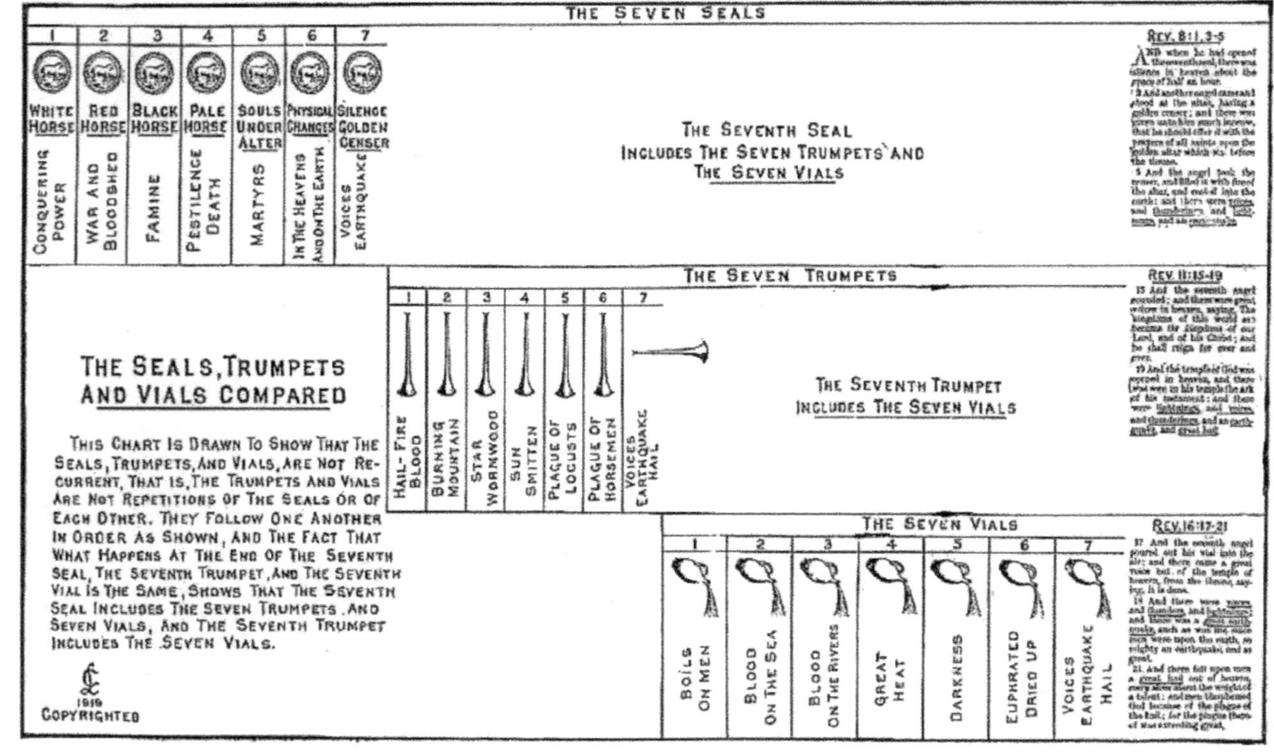
THE SEVEN SEALS
1 WHITE HORSE CONQUERING POWER
2 RED HORSE WAR AND BLOODSHED
3 BLACK HORSE FAMINE
4 PALE HORSE PESTILENCE DEATH
5 SOULS UNDER ALTER MARTYRS
6 PHYSICAL CHANGES IN THE HEAVENS AND ON THE EARTH
7 SILENCE GOLDEN CENSER VOICES EARTHQUAKE
THE SEVENTH SEAL INCLUDES THE SEVEN TRUMPETS AND THE SEVEN VIALS
REV. 8:1, 3-5
THE SEVEN TRUMPETS
1 HAIL- FIRE BLOOD
2 BURNING MOUNTAIN
3 STAR WORMWOOD
4 SUN SMITTEN
5 PLAGUE OF LOCUSTS
6 PLAGUE OF HORSEMEN
7 VOICES EARTHQUAKE HAIL
THE SEVENTH TRUMPET INCLUDES THE SEVEN VIALS
REV. 11:15-19
THE SEVEN VIALS
1 BOILS ON MEN
2 BLOOD ON THE SEA
3 BLOOD ON THE RIVERS
4 GREAT HEAT
5 DARKNESS
6 EUPHRATED DRIED UP
7 VOICES EARTHQUAKE HAIL
REV. 16:17-21
THE SEALS, TRUMPETS AND VIALS COMPARED
THIS CHART IS DRAWN TO SHOW THAT THE SEALS, TRUMPETS, AND VIALS, ARE NOT RE-CURRENT, THAT IS, THE TRUMPETS AND VIALS ARE NOT REPETITIONS OF THE SEALS OR OF EACH OTHER. THEY FOLLOW ONE ANOTHER IN ORDER AS SHOWN, AND THE FACT THAT WHAT HAPPENS AT THE END OF THE SEVENTH SEAL, THE SEVENTH TRUMPET, AND THE SEVENTH VIAL IS THE SAME, SHOWS THAT THE SEVENTH SEAL INCLUDES THE SEVEN TRUMPETS, AND SEVEN VIALS, AND THE SEVENTH TRUMPET INCLUDES THE SEVEN VIALS.
1919
COPYRIGHTED

Judgment of the Systems

John the Apostle, still connected into the Lords streaming vision realm, as he not only sees another angel, but one of them speaks to him as well. I truly believe John is actually sitting in the viewing room, in heaven. Now he (John) is really a chosen one! So, let us now look at chapters 17 and 18; and how prophecy continues to come forth with the foretelling of judgment. When one looks at the overall outcome of what is to take place in these two chapters, it is very clear of what will happen.

Revelation: Chapter 17

Prophetically it is the destruction of the *political systems*, *commercial systems* and *religious systems* of *Babylon the Great*, *The Mother of Harlots*. Here it is… There were *seven kings*, which probably refer to the *seven world empires*, which influenced human government throughout history – Egypt, Assyria, *Babylon*, Medo-Persia, Greece and Rome. What are the things that came out of "Babylon the Great"?

- All idolatrous religion
- Greed-based commerce
- Secular government began there

As this continues they (the Beast and his followers) will make war with the *Lamb*, and how will this occur? It will occur when these (ten kings) kill His (God's) faithful followers and come out to fight against Christ in the “Battle of Armageddon”! Those who join (will you be one of them) with Christ to overcome them, called “chosen and faithful”…

Would you like to know more?

Revelation: Chapter 18

Prophetically this chapter begins with the words "*after these things*", which (John the Apostle) saw. What did he see? The things recorded in the previous chapter, the destruction of "Babylon the Great". What is this destruction? It is the judgment on the commercial, governmental and religious systems that originated there. Who else saw this judgment in the fulfillment of this prophecy? No other than the prophet Isaiah 47:1-9 (cf. Isa. 21-9). In these systems, which the commercial, social, and political systems of the Antichrist will receive double judgment for their sins. This chapter is summed up by the angel of God casting a millstone into the sea as an example of how the kingdom of the Antichrist, is destroyed in that moment. This judgment will definitely target those who, while they lived in and on the earth traded their soul for material possession.

Would you like to know more?

The Triumphant Praise and His Return

As the last chapters of 19, 20, 21, and 22 in the Book of Revelation ends, each chapter brings forth prophetic revelation in a magnificent manner. As we look at chapter 19, John the Apostle is still receiving his vision stream, and he is still hearing the voice of the Lord. This event is undoubtedly one of the most dramatic events in the entire Bible! What we find is the Church, the "Bride of Christ", who is the guest of honor at the marriage of the Lamb in heaven; and returns with Christ in His triumphal "*Second Coming*" in a most awesome way! All born again believers should shout, right now!

John the Apostle true prophetic vision reveals this in chapter 19:

- Praise in Heaven
- The awesome Marriage of the Lamb
- The Glorious Appearing of Jesus Christ on a white horse

As chapter 19 ends, we see that *the beast*... and ... *the false prophet* begin to meet their doom by Jesus Christ casting them "alive into a lake of fire". Out of all, these are the first two that are casted into it. These two men do not go to judgment; rather they go straight to "Hell", eternal punishment they will receive and endure forever (cf. Rev. 20:10).

Now as we begin in chapter 20, John the Apostle saw an angel descend down from heaven, having the "key of the bottomless pit". Could this be the same angel in (Rev. 9:1) given the key to the same bottomless pit stated here? I believe it is. The angel is about to lock an inescapable prison cell where there is no escape! Therefore, this chapter introduces Christ's Millennial Kingdom, which begins with the beast (Satan) and the false prophet, thrown in the bottomless pit and Satan is bound for a thousand years.

John the Apostle true prophetic vision reveals this in chapter 20:

1. The bottomless pit (is simply the Abyss) where evil spirits reside

2. The key shows authority

3. The chain depicts imprisonment and binding

4. John the Apostle saw "thrones", which represents the administration of the messianic kingdom, divine government and judgment

5. The book of life contains the name of every person who has received eternal life through faith alone

As chapter 20 ends, we see God take one last look at the "book of life" during the "Great White Throne Judgment"; He skims over it for a final check of those names of anyone at this final judgment is there. The word of God says if your name is not written in the book according to what John the Apostle saw regarding the book openings (he did not see the names), you will be cast into the lake of fire.

Now as we see in chapter 21 and 22 John the Apostle continues to see in his vision a description of the eternal state following the Millennium and the final judgment that surrounds the New Jerusalem as the eternal habitation of the saved. So, what will be some of the newness of the new heaven and new earth?

John the Apostle true prophetic vision reveals this in chapter 21:

1. The prophet Isaiah foretold the new heaven and new earth (cf. Is. 65:17; 66:22)

2. The present universe will be cleansed of all the effects of sin (cf. 2 Pet. 3:7, 10-13)

3. When Jesus ascended to His Father's house, this is where He was building the mansion for His bride, the Church (cf. John 14:1-4). This is prophetic because the fulfilling of it is after the Millennium; Christ will bring that "city" to the new beautified earth where He will setup His capital for eternity. Now, can you see why we are all temporary citizens on this old earth?

4. It is done: The eternal purpose of God to gather a Holy, devoted people to himself has now been accomplished

5. He is Alpha (the beginning – God is the origin and source of all things cf. Is. 41:4; 44:6; 48:12) and Omega (the end – God is also the goal or aim of all things cf. Rom. 10:4)

6. The water of life represents eternal sustenance and provision

7. The gold and precious stones may be earthly materials glorified (cf. 1 Cor. 15:50-54)

8. There is no temple in the city, since both the Father and the Son will be present in their fullest manifestations

John the Apostle true prophetic vision reveals this in chapter 22:

1. There will be abundant life and continuous blessings

2. One river, containing water of life which comes from God's throne

3. The healing of nations truly comes forth

4. The effects of the Post-Eden or (Edenic) curse from (cf. Gen. 3:14-19) will be totally gone forever

5. God's saints will server Him (cf. Rev. 7:15) and reign with Him forever (cf. Dan. 7:18, 27)

As chapter 22 closes and the summary of the Book of Revelation ends. There are two themes emphasized: (1) the prophetic agenda, and the authenticity of the Book of Revelation from God; and (2) the imminence of the return of Christ. These sayings refer to the entire Book of Revelation. All authenticated as genuine through His holy prophets, and by the angel whom God sent to give them through John the Apostle to His servants, that is, the members, the Churches. Here it is... Jesus said... (*Quickly* – here refers to the imminence of the "Rapture" or "Caught Up" can occur "*at any time*" of the Church in (cf. Rev. 22:7). Amen

Conclusion

God Why Did You Reveal This Too Me

I end the closing of this prophetic night vision with the following … I totally believe that the Lord thy God revealed this prophetic night vision to me because… 1. We are living in the last days, and He truly is now pouring out His spirit on His sons and daughters for them to prophesy, have visions and dream, dreams. 2. He can trust a true prophet to disseminate out the truth of this prophetic night vision with specific details to the Body of Christ and the world, and… 3. Have the passion to bring life to this true night vision event.

However, there will be many unbelievers of Jesus Christ and God, which will question the authenticity of this prophetic night vision and dream, and especially the Book of Revelation not to be true in its content and or context.

The Revelation of Jesus Christ by John the Apostle: The key scripture is verse 3. The blessing of verse 3 has a threefold condition.

1) *Read* the book…

2) *Hear* (understand and obtain divine revelation) from it, and …

3) *Keep* and (obey) it.

> [1] *The Revelation of Jesus Christ, which God gave unto him, to shew unto his servants things which must shortly come to pass; and he sent and signified it by his angel unto his servant John:*
>
> [2] *Who bare record of the Word of God, and of the testimony of Jesus Christ, and of all things that he saw.*
>
> [3] *Blessed is he that readeth, and they that hear the words of this prophecy, and keep those things which are written therein: for the time is at hand.*

Revelation 1:1-3 KJV – Read the AMP version as well

May the Lord thy God bless all those who read this book.

CAUGHT UP

Night Vision Revealed

ARE YOU PREPARED?

About the Author

Mark D Watt has a solid foundation for preaching, teaching of the Word of God, visions, and dreams because of the prophetic anointing that is on his life. For additional information, or if you would like to invite Mark to speak, please contact him.

Write to:

Mark D Watt

Caught Up Night Vision Revealed

P.O. Box 1090

Wake Forest, NC 27588

USA

You can visit his website, get in touch, or obtain more online at –

www.caughtupnightvisionrevealed.com

www.caughtupnightvisionrevealed.info

www.facebook.com/caughtupnightvisionrevealed

https://twitter.com/CaughtUpNiteVis

www.ingramcontent.com/pod-product-compliance
Lightning Source LLC
Chambersburg PA
CBHW031955040426
42448CB00006B/362

* 9 7 8 0 6 1 5 8 9 1 4 5 3 *